MW00573425

GEN Z

REGINA LUTTRELL
and
KAREN McGRATH

GEN Z

THE
SUPERHERO
GENERATION

ROWMAN & LITTLEFIELD
Lanham • Boulder • New York • London

Published by Rowman & Littlefield
An imprint of The Rowman & Littlefield Publishing Group, Inc.
4501 Forbes Boulevard, Suite 200, Lanham, Maryland 20706
www.rowman.com

6 Tinworth Street, London SE11 5AL, United Kingdom

British Library Cataloguing in Publication Information Available

Library of Congress Cataloging-in-Publication Data

Names: Luttrell, Regina, 1975– author. | McGrath, Karen, 1965– author.
Title: Gen Z : the superhero generation / Regina Luttrell and Karen McGrath.
Description: Lanham, Maryland : Rowman & Littlefield, [2021] | Includes
    bibliographical references and index.
Identifiers: LCCN 2020054104 (print) | LCCN 2020054105 (ebook) | ISBN
    9781538127988 (cloth) | ISBN 9781538127995 (epub)
Subjects: LCSH: Generation Z. | Generation Z—Social life and customs. |
    Generation Z—Attitudes. | Young adults. | Intergenerational relations.
Classification: LCC HQ799.5 .L86 2021 (print) | LCC HQ799.5 (ebook) | DDC
    305.23—dc23
LC record available at https://lccn.loc.gov/2020054104
LC ebook record available at https://lccn.loc.gov/2020054105

"Go in peace, my daughter. And remember that, in a world of ordinary mortals, you are a Wonder Woman."—Queen Hippolyte

Dedicated to my superheroes: Emma and Avery

CONTENTS

CONTENTS

ACKNOWLEDGMENTS

"Have you ever seen a little girl run so far she falls down? There's an instant, a fraction of a second before the world catches hold of her again. . . . A moment when she's outrun every doubt and fear she's ever had about herself and she flies. In that one moment, every little girl flies."—Captain Marvel

REGINA LUTTRELL

Superheroes never work alone. They have a strong support system that allows them to do their work and save the day. So do I. I am often asked how I can do so much—from being a wife and mother to researching, writing, and teaching. My answer is always the same. I could not accomplish an iota of what I am able to without the eternal support of my best friend and husband, Todd. He is my biggest fan and my personal superhero. Because of you, I am that little girl who can outrun her fears and fly. Here's to you, my caped crusader!

Every superhero needs a partner, and for me that's Karen. Thank you for going on every adventure with me, for keeping me sane with your witty jokes, for your continued loyalty, and for persevering through every book we write and every project we collaborate on.

KAREN MCGRATH

Writing a book is not an easy task, but there are ways to make that process flow a bit better, and it starts with those around you. Thank you to the College of Saint Rose, the School of Arts and Humanities, and my Communications Department colleagues for the sabbatical opportunity and support to pursue this project.

I would also like to thank my coauthor and friend, Regina (Gina) Luttrell, for having confidence in me and taking me on this wild ride. You have always been a great friend and colleague whose passion and expertise motivate those around you—especially me. I thank you for the opportunities we have had to develop our scholarship together and strengthen our friendship at the same time. You are a forever friend, and I am blessed to have you in my life. I also thank my family for believing in me even when I get snarky and overwhelmed, which happens a lot! I thank Luna (my cat) for being my writing buddy and leg warmer during this writing process and always. Most importantly, however, I thank my partner and love of my life, Sean, for being my emotional, mental, and physical rock. Your unconditional love and support mean more to me than any amount of words can capture: I love you!

Remembering some of our superheroes:

William Cozenza
Laura Dremann
John Fisher
Caroline and Frank Franco
Rita and Thomas Heyer
Theresa Macchia
Susan Mare
Kathy Walsh

FOREWORD

I have been challenging colleagues and peers to answer a question: Do you ever know how someone feels? Asking "How do you feel?" especially in a business setting is much more personal sounding. More commonly, "How are you?" appears in daily conversations and is asked casually, whether you know a person or not.

Being in marketing and PR for thirty-plus years is an educational journey in communication signals. You learn to read signs deciphering how someone feels, which is not as easy as it seems. Whether written communication, including the tweets you see on Twitter and the tone of voice wrapped around these messages, to the spoken word and resulting body language, you have to be fully aware to recognize what is coming at you. Signals present themselves all the time and with social media, they are fast and furious. Are you taking the time to decode these signals before you communicate?

As you look at the hundreds of thousands of messages from friends, colleagues, family members, and acquaintances flowing in through all your channels, somewhere in the message, whether directly or indirectly, overtly or not, they are sharing their feelings. Of course, as trust in your relationships deepen, the messages become more evident, or you begin to read between the lines as you get to know someone better.

I have shared publicly, both on stage and on social media, how a twenty-four-year-old millennial placed me on the path to FEEL. After my stepdaughter passed away in September 2018, I wanted to understand the younger generation and how they communicated. I have always viewed social media as a highlight reel of the best moments showcasing smiles with family and friends. However, there was never a more crucial time for me to question how the people around me were feeling versus what they were sharing in their online social communities. For all of us, it is time to take notice by being present and more mindful and by truly listening with our ears; eyes; and, most of all, our hearts.

For as much as people on social media are willing to share their most exceptional experiences, aspirations, motivations, and even their frustrations and rants, I started to recognize different identities surface. As a member of Gen-X, I have been counseling working professionals saying, "Who you are online is who you are off-line." However, younger professionals and students were not always finding their paths to one identity. It looked as if this was becoming increasingly more difficult.

It was after a fifty-two-plus-week research study speaking with millennials for the bulk of my interviews, as well as members of Gen-Z, that I started to learn a lot more about these younger, hopeful, passionate, and driven individuals. My eyes opened to insights and in-depth perspectives that were not necessarily part of their matching online persona(s). Then, after conducting some social media research using the Talkwalker Quick Search tool, I noticed immediately what younger generations were asking for from the people they looked up to was not always present in their interactions.

What stood out the most was that they did not feel as if the people around them, whether in their companies or their social media communities, were always open and inclusive. They wanted to be heard, and they also wanted people from diverse backgrounds to be recognized. When asked about building relationships, it was the lack of empathy they witnessed on social media and not enough caring and kindness at their jobs that prevented the growth of these connections into anything meaningful or long-term.

Being in communications and PR for so many years, I was not shocked to learn the younger generation did not think their leaders were accurate, transparent, or honest at times, especially on social media. Within their own companies, they also questioned why leaders don't trust us with the truth.

Especially, today with so much uncertainty in the economy, businesses, politics, climate change, the health-care system, and a global pandemic, telling it like it is is more important and appreciated by younger generations.

Their passions surface when a cause is focused on the environment and saving the planet. Sustainability, human rights, animal rights, and several other topics have younger generations looking for the companies who care—from where they'll find employment to the brands that deserve their business.

What surfaced from the conversations and social media research were four distinct areas, or buckets, I called FEEL (fears, empathy, ethics, love). The FEEL model was born because younger generations are looking for others to FEEL as much as they do. They want others to be open and inclusive (facing *fears*) and have kindness and compassion (engaging with *empathy*). They are looking for people who exercise good judgment and demonstrate values (using *ethics*) and surround themselves with people who show as much passion as these young, opinionated superstars (unleashing the *love*).

FEEL is a lens for communication, relationships, and memorable experiences with trusted confidants. Yes, FEEL started with a millennial and was built mostly by millennials. However, the communication approach sets the foundation for younger generations like Gen-Z and, perhaps, other generations to come because FEEL is the most human way to interact and build deeper bonds. What millennials started the Gen-Z superheroes will drive home using their distinctive talents in the "digiverse." They will make FEEL a part of their super journeys, as they educate others along the way.

Authors Regina Luttrell and Karen McGrath poignantly state how Generation Z has superhero-like characteristics, yet they clearly state that they do not have superhuman powers. They are not proclaiming that Gen-Zers are godlike superheroes; instead, they acknowledge that the role of technology in their lives has assisted them in creating and engaging the world in unique ways, so much so that they, too, can be perceived as superhero-like.

For years I have shared with professional peers how younger generations are our future leaders. What we invest now in the growth and development of these superheroes, whether it is mentoring or sponsoring them in our organizations, will be reflective in our world in years to come. If these superheroes are willing to step outside their comfort zones, showing up for their causes with sheer determination while teaching other generations to live with passion, then I am all for joining their cause. Of course, bringing FEEL into all our interactions and through all our channels is a movement that I would personally and professionally like to see these superheroes ignite. As they are out changing the world, believing, and doing well by doing good, Gen-Z naturally adds FEEL to their experiences and accomplishments.

If you want to learn how and why Gen-Z is a standout and stand-up generation, then you will want to read this book. As for my PR and marketing friends and business colleagues, this book is definitely for you. A big thank-you to the authors for researching, identifying, and sharing how Gen-Z will become a generation to watch as their superhero-like powers unfold.

Although every generation has its stereotypes and is often criticized (with good intentions) by earlier generations, Gen-Z will not disappoint. Whether they are in the digiverse or wherever they show up with FEEL in tow, I'll be there, cheering them along!

Deirdre Breakenridge
CEO, Pure Performance Communications

PREFACE

We can't believe it has been five years since we published *The Millennial Mindset: Unraveling Fact from Fiction*. Yet here we are, bringing you our take on Generation Z (Gen-Z)—what we have labeled the "superhero generation." We believe it is important to discuss this generation now because they are already having an impact in our homes, workplaces, and classrooms. As we look to the future, we need to understand better who they are and what motivates them to succeed.

Why the superhero generation, you ask? Superheroes are often defined as courageous, powerful, virtuous, and strong. Equipped with unique special powers, these individuals stand up for what is right, battling supervillains to ensure that good prevails and all is well in the world. We live in turbulent times, where religious, political, and economic barriers weigh heavy. Where invasions and war are rampant around the globe. Where true equality is known for only a select few. Where the environment is under attack. And where pandemics have emerged once again as a real concern.

Gen-Zers have an uphill battle to right the world and save the earth. Their nemeses and supervillains appear in the shapes of humans, ideologies, and facts, conflicting at their core. We believe that, just as early comic book superheroes enabled reflection, discussion, and debate, today's superheroes stem from current world events and injustices that must be addressed by Gen-Z.

In this book, we identify six prominent superhero characteristics and explain how Gen-Zers reflect these characteristics in their daily lives. For us, Gen-Z is a superhero-like generation affected by technology, education, and world events. As the latest generation to make an impact on society, they have the world and our future in their hands.

To make our case, we examined resources and studies and conducted our own survey to grasp how people perceive Gen-Z. In the following chapters, we share our results with you. We provide a structured overview of previous generations and explain a bit about superheroes in popular culture. Then we direct your attention to the superhero characteristics Gen-Zers exhibit and highlight how these characteristics can be leveraged in the classroom and the workplace. To conclude, we offer suggestions to parents, teachers, coworkers, employers, and Gen-Zers for moving forward and connecting with each other.

As you reflect on these characteristics, you may notice how previous generations have similar characteristics in different forms. Technological advances, such as the Internet and social media platforms, coupled with world events primed this generation to don its capes for just causes, and many are only now realizing that their roles can be impactful from early childhood and throughout their lives.

The meteoric rise of superheroes in the past two decades provides Gen-Z fodder for taking a stand and using their superhero powers. Mistakes will be made, but snow-plow parents must allow this superhero generation to learn from those mistakes while also preparing them to become active, communicatively capable citizens who can engage in civilized discourse and behavior with presumed human, ideological, or factual (sometimes alternative-factual) villains or opponents. So, in the words of Captain America,

> Doesn't matter what the press says. Doesn't matter what the politicians or the mobs say. Doesn't matter if the whole country decides that something wrong is something right. This nation was founded on one principle above all else: the requirement that we stand up for what we believe, no matter the odds or the consequences. When the mob and the press and the world tell you to move, your job is to plant yourself like a tree beside the river of truth, and tell the whole world—"No, you move."[1]

I

CHARACTERIZING GEN-Z

The Superhero Generation

1

THE GENERATIONS

Traditionalists, Boomers, Gen-X, and Millennials

"I know how hard it is when everything we know to be true changes. But sometimes all we can do is just accept the way things are, and make the best of that."—Supergirl

DISTINCT GENERATIONS

Having raised, taught, and regularly interacted with Gen-Zers, we have experienced firsthand this generation. We know all too well what makes them tick. We have had a front-row seat to unraveling historical events that have shaped their experiences, watched beliefs turn into principles, and been part of the progression from childhood to adulthood. Understanding who this generation is can illuminate how they affect our homes, workplaces, and classrooms. This chapter delves into the characteristics of four prior generations: traditionalists, baby boomers, Generation X, and millennials. We identify who they are, what they have accomplished, and what they expect from others.

GENERATIONAL CHARACTERISTICS

The historical events that formed our beliefs, behaviors, values, and attitudes assist us in understanding how each generation is influenced and shaped.[1] A generation is defined by a specific persona: the aspect of someone's character that is presented to others.[2] People of a generation grow up in a particular era and share similar experiences during the first twenty to twenty-three years of their lives. Generations can be longer or shorter, depending on the historical events and experiences that occur during this formative time.[3]

Perhaps surprisingly, defining a generation is more of an approximation rather than a hard, scientific calculation. Perceived membership, shared beliefs and behaviors, and a common location in history are the three attributes associated with the makeup of any generation.[4] Our generational personas and characteristics influence our decisions and life choices. Because identifying generational personas is not a science, a person may not have all the characteristics that define their generation. At times, some people will identify with a generation they are not technically part of. Regardless, we must come to recognize each generation separately and collectively so we can gain the necessary insights to understand how they are connected and form the generations that follow.

We are more diverse than at any other time in history. The Census Bureau reports that the population in the United States will become a minority majority by 2045.[5] Their data reveals that the White population will decrease by 10 percent between now and 2060, while the African American population will grow 58 percent, the Hispanic population will increase by 89 percent, and the Asian population by 111 percent during that same time period.[6] This growing diversity brings about people from various cultural groups, religions, and ethnicities. In *The Millennial Mindset*, we point out that increased diversity was being seen just about everywhere: within our community settings, classrooms, and work environments.[7] We know that diversity leads to better communication, feelings of connectedness, and distinct societal and cultural shifts.

Properly identifying with these generational personas and their attitudes about "family life, gender roles, institutions, politics, religion, culture, lifestyle, and the future" can be valuable for successfully integrating the ideals and goals of various generational groups.[8] Because historical events have also shaped the beliefs, behaviors, values, and attitudes of a generation, it is important to acknowledge and leverage differences in developing interpersonal relationships.

Let us now look at each of the prior generations so that we can establish their connection to Gen-Zers. An abbreviated version of each generation's attributes is outlined in this chapter. This content is based on materials from *The Millennial Mindset* and is offered here as a review. Understanding how prior generational personas were formed helps us recognize the impact they have on future generations, such as Generation Z: the Superhero Generation.

The Traditionalists Generation: 1927–1945

This generation, also known as traditionalists, are presently in their late seventies into their early eighties. Nearly all traditionalists are retired from the workforce, and those who remain work few hours and have little involvement with the youngest groups of employees: millennials and Gen-Zers.[9] Traditionalists are perceived to be thrifty, hardworking, and respectful of authority and duty—especially to their country and employer—before pleasure. Although members of this generation are largely retired, traditionalists remain connected, influential, and affluent.[10] In other words, they are still relevant in this ever-evolving world. To better understand how history has helped shape the traditionalists' generational persona, it is helpful to highlight some of the major events that occurred during their upbringing.

The traditionalists grew up in an era bookended by two world wars. Radio and print periodicals were the main source of media, people were starting to concern themselves with such topics as workplace safety and child labor laws, and consumer independence became an important feature of the culture, as evidenced by the birth of the Piggly Wiggly supermarket in Memphis in 1916.[11] Additionally, the advent of cinematic films, including D. W. Griffith's *Birth of a Nation*, influenced the norms and expectations of diverse and underrepresented groups.

At the time, the government limited consumer choices of health care and alcohol consumption (Prohibition), and morality was on trial, as evolution or creationism was debated in the Scopes trial of 1925.[12] Despite some governmental influence on the general public's behaviors, (White) women were dutifully given the right to vote in 1920 with the Nineteenth Amendment.[13] The generations immediately preceding the traditionalists had clearly defined racial and gender roles, experienced some technological advancements, and thrived economically, but this was much different for traditionalists.

The conclusion of World War I paved the way for a strong national economy, providing many middle-class Americans with an increased living standard. During this time, Wall Street was also thriving, and the value of US currency was holding strong around the world—until the market crash of 1929 and the resulting Great Depression.[14] Post–World War I economic comfort was replaced with bread lines, severe unemployment, and poverty for those not in the upper echelon of society. With a second world war approaching, this generation embraced the idea of *earning your place* in the world. Constant fears around the globe in the latter part of the traditionalist era provides us with some insight as to how the United States was positioning itself for the future.

At the close of the Great Depression and into the latter part of the traditionalist era, accepted gender roles held strong. Men worked outside the home (or were at war), while a growing number of women worked in industries that supported the war effort, including aviation and uniform manufacturing. Rosie the Riveter emerged as one of the iconic female images prevalent to the era.[15] However, non-Whites (e.g., Native Americans, Mexicans, Puerto Ricans, Chinese) struggled with racism despite the abolition of slavery and improved immigration and citizenship laws. Migrant workers from Central and South American countries worked the fields but lived in deplorable conditions and were paid less than a livable wage. Native Americans, who still struggled for rights and citizenship, were often used in the war effort, especially as code breakers, and their skills directly assisted the victory. Jim Crow laws were prominent, despite the large number of African American men, including the Tuskegee Airmen, supporting the war effort.[16] Sex and sexuality were often thought about and portrayed in the language of reproduction, Christianity, and morality, while lesbians and gay men remained closeted during their service to the country's war effort. Diversity was feared and condemned, which continued into the early baby boom era.

Traditionalists' life experiences shaped their behaviors, attitudes, and beliefs. Fears of difference and a lack of understanding of economics set the tone for a continued national identity and contributed to the social identity of this generation. As a witness to the Great Depression, traditionalists consider work a privilege and firmly believe that individuals climb the corporate ladder through hard work. Leaders from this generation prefer a top-down management style and expect others to conform. Traditionalists feel they are respected and valued for their experience. They believe that long hours at work, from 8:00 a.m. to 5:00 p.m., should be the norm, and they often consider weekends *company time*, not *family time*.[17] They are fiercely loyal and have spent most of their careers working only with one or two employers.

Traditionalists oversaw the introduction of the atomic bomb, fluorescent light bulbs, FM radios, gasoline-powered lawn mowers, penicillin, bubblegum, and ballpoint pens and also survived the Second World War.[18] After the war, the men of this generation still worked outside the home, while the wives tended to the family unit. Growing up in this era exposed them to a number of life-defining experiences. As a result, traditionalists can be highly demanding and are often the most technologically challenged of the generations that we discuss.

There is some movement toward technology as the coronavirus (COVID-19) has forced social distancing and isolation.[19] Now we are assisting traditionalists in learning how to Facetime, Skype, use Facebook Live, and other virtual apps. These individuals prefer a brick-and-mortar educational experience with a conventional professor-led lecture rather than online or web-based educational models. Traditionalists continue to struggle to adopt new technologies and work processes, and who can blame them? Yet because of their loyalty, affluence, and values, they remain important to more established corporations, political organizations, and industries. As a result, parents and guardians who grew up during this era had a profound influence on their own children: the baby boomers.

The Baby Boom Generation: 1946–1964

Baby boomers, or boomers, are characterized as opportunistic, possessing a strong work ethic, and open to challenging the status quo of the traditional gender roles within education and the workplace. Boomers are responsible for both the first generation of educated women working side by side with men and the establishment of dual-career parents. Work truly defines this generation. Baby boomers rely on the belief that their self-worth is tied directly to their work ethic. Right or wrong, they often judge others based on this principle, as well. These individuals see the work-life balance as a nicety but not truly achievable. Understandably, this can cause great tension between this generation and younger ones in the workforce.[20]

Boomers are remembered for their propensity to question authority, ushering in the *nuclear family* unit, and indulging in affluent lifestyle behaviors, which has led to them being labeled the me generation.[21] Burning flags and draft cards while fleeing to Canada to avoid the Vietnam War, hippies, bell-bottom jeans, long hair, liberal political views, rock 'n' roll, noncommittal sexual encounters, the pill, recreational drugs, confronting authority, credit cards, television, and even Tupperware are among the images that come to mind when we think about the boomers.[22] To understand how these circumstances and views came to be, we need to take a closer look at some of the major events and changes that this generation experienced.

On both a personal and professional level, this generation is particularly comfortable with bucking the common trend and walking away from long-standing relationships that no longer suit their needs. Boomers are accepting of divorce and have an increased likelihood of working for multiple companies. Making up 30 percent of the US population, boomers represent a large portion of management positions in corporate America and may choose to work part time during their retirement.[23]

This generation embodies experimentation and an unconventional way of thinking. Soldiers returning from World War II tried to reestablish themselves within American societies, expecting that they would return to their normal, prewar lives. The Cold War accelerated during this era with the threat of communism and the United States stepping into its role as a world superpower. The United States also faced many social changes during this time, including challenges to racial, sexual, and gender barriers.

The close of World War II drove substantial economic growth in the United States as the memory of the Great Depression disappeared. Children born in 1945, the start of the baby boom, grew up during a time of technology advances and prosperity, as the value of the dollar increased. Companies begin to take greater advantage of advertising, which shaped America's views on commerce. Spending increased with the introduction of the credit card, and perceptions of money began to change. Financially speaking, boomers saw an opportunity to seize each moment and delay payment rather than delaying their gratification as the traditionalists had done. Although some economic recessions occurred during this time, the boomer era is generally characterized as one of sustained economic growth.[24] Much like the emergence of the supermarket, this generation saw the emergence of the first fast food restaurants (e.g., McDonald's) and the establishment of a national highway system to keep up with the changing pace of life and recreational desires.

As the first African American player in Major League Baseball (MLB), Jackie Robinson faced countless racial barriers on and off the field when he broke the baseball color line and started at first base for the Brooklyn Dodgers in 1947. This act of bravery, not only by Robinson, but also the entire Dodger organization, proved successful, as evidenced by the racial diversity observed in Major League Baseball and other sports leagues today.

As substantial as this step was toward establishing racial equality within sports, many other events surfaced during the boomer era. *Brown v. the Board of Education* (1954) resulted in the Supreme Court's decision to integrate schools, thus declaring segregation of schools unconstitutional. This case helped pave the way for the courts to overturn *Plessy v. Ferguson* (1896), and unjust laws, especially Jim Crow laws in the South, and racial discrimination in general would become less tolerated and accepted.[25]

During this era, the United States experienced a number of other racial equality battles highlighted by the Montgomery Bus Boycott of 1955, the Little Rock Nine in 1957, and the emergence of nonviolent protester Martin Luther King Jr. (MLK) as an opponent to the police use of force. Support for the civil rights movement culminated with an August 1963 Civil Rights March on Washington, DC, for jobs and freedom, with 250,000 demonstrators, including President John F. Kennedy (JFK), assembling in the National Mall.

This generation also saw the official end to Jim Crow laws in 1964 and a continued swell of the civil rights movement. Although the discrimination of African Americans was the focus of demonstrations during this period, members of other races experienced similar levels of discrimination. Many of these discriminated groups began to advocate for the rights of all people, thus promoting broader acceptance of gender, racial, and sexual differences within society and giving rise to the lesbian, gay, bisexual, and transgender (LGBT) rights movement of the late 1960s.

This era also brought about a shift in gender equality—or inequality. Many women were not interested in returning to their prewar roles, so they fought for expanded rights, often paralleling the civil right movement in many ways. Sexual freedom was directly addressed with the controversial introduction of the pill to the pharmaceutical market in 1960, raising questions about morality and promiscuity among young women while also presenting the possibility of sex for pleasure rather than for reproduction. Premarital sex debates increased during the mid- to late 1960s with the push for *free love*. Betty Friedan published *Feminine Mystique* in 1964, which led to the development of the National Organization for Women (NOW) in 1966. There was also the Second Wave of Feminism, which challenged cultural gender assumptions: "The so-called Youth Revolution of the 1960s, for example, produced rapid changes in behavior, clothing music, entertainment, even social and sexual manner (or rather their absence)."[26] This was a time of progressive change, all under the watchful eye of a supportive president who was integral to the expansion of the rights of so many different groups.

With television sets becoming increasingly affordable and prominent, radio programming was on the decline, and many politicians struggled to adjust to this new technology that emphasized one's appearance and charisma. One can believe that Franklin D. Roosevelt may not have experienced as much political success during this era because US citizens would have seen his weakness: his use of a wheelchair. However, we can also see how effective this medium was for other individuals. John F. Kennedy was a young, handsome man with a beautiful wife, and his charisma made for great television, especially during his televised presidential debate with Richard Nixon, who ultimately struggled with this new medium.

While television brought us an increase in advertising and programming sponsors, it also provided us images of Americans in space and indirectly led to the resurgence of the nuclear family after World War II. Television would be quite prominent and impactful for years to come, while radio would be pressed into finding a new entertainment outlet in music—thus the emergence of crossover legend Elvis Presley. The combination of Elvis's music, good looks, and hips brought much concern from baby boomers' parents: His music was far reaching, bringing together all races and challenging Jim Crow laws and segregation.

Additionally, the environment became a topic of concern during this era, highlighted by the 1962 publication of *Silent Spring* by Rachel Carson. In her book, Carson, a well-known biologist, ecologist, and author, "exposed the hazards of the pesticide DDT, eloquently questioned humanity's faith in technological progress and helped set the stage for the environmental movement."[27] The release of Carson's book, in part, and a parallel environmental movement promoted awareness of this important topic throughout all societies.

In retrospect, we can see that the baby boom generation experienced closure of the last world war, an economic renewal, a push for civil rights and equality, humanitarian efforts, the mainstreaming of new media, and the rise of environmental awareness. This era experienced an ideological shift from what the country and government can do to help the people to what people can do to help their country and government. The events of this generation influenced the beliefs, behaviors, values, and attitudes of so many baby boomers today and ultimately played a pivotal role in the next generation: Generation X.

Generation X: 1965-1980

Generation X, also commonly referred to as Gen-X, is flanked by two larger generations—the predominantly White baby boomers and the highly diverse millennials.[28] We can learn more about the beliefs, behaviors, values, and attitudes of this generation by taking a look at some historical events that helped define them.

In a broad sense, Gen-X is the first generation that experienced significant corporate downsizing, enormous layoffs, broad economic challenges, and widespread governmental scandals. Children often grew up in double-income, divorced family units. According to a 2004 study conducted by the marketing strategy and research firm Reach Advisors, Gen-Xers are seen as a neglected generation; their formative years fell within "one of the least parented, least nurtured generations in U.S. history."[29] This generation was the first to be raised in day cares, and nearly 40 percent were considered "latchkey kids." As a result, it should not be a surprise that this generation is very independent, resourceful, and enterprising by nature.

Gen-Xers place family first and strive for optimum work-life balance. They are involved in all aspects of their children's lives, and they are ferocious advocates who demand power and decision-making rights to ensure that their children receive what they need.[30] In fact, Amazon founder Jeff

Bezos, Google founders Sergey Brin and Larry Page, and the founders of YouTube are all Gen-Xers.

Those born during the earlier part of this generation grew up while the United States was involved in the Vietnam conflict and the subsequent societal protests about whether this was a *war* or simply *police action*. Many baby boomers, the parents of Gen-Xers, fought the draft and became activists during the 1960s. Early Gen-Xers either experienced firsthand, read about, or heard about many history-shaping events, including Martin Luther King Jr.'s assassination, riots at the 1968 Democratic National Convention in Chicago, tensions between students and the National Guard at Kent State University in 1970, the Watergate hearings, an energy crisis, a presidential resignation, and gay rights debates encompassing the entire political spectrum.

Also, more than any previous generation, Gen-Xers are comfortable with technological advances and diversity and have an appreciation for global issues. They are the first generation to grow up with CDs, remote controls, cell phones, e-mail, fax machines, computers, and the Internet. Gen-Xers contribute to the workplace as independent, resourceful, and self-sufficient individuals who value both freedom and responsibility. They seek out fun yet meaningful workplaces and dislike conformity, so much that if they feel boxed in or pigeonholed, Gen-Xers will not think twice about finding a new employer.[31] Gen-Xers flourish when they are challenged and are given creative freedom and autonomy.[32] This generation also values the freedom to set their own work hours and the ability to work from home when possible. Eager and ambitious to learn new skills, Gen-Xers crave training that relates to their overall careers and seek instruction that is interactive and computer based. While working in groups is accepted, individuals from this generation prefer to work using a more hands-off approach when supervising or mentoring others.

As this generation was coming of age, President Nixon began to worry about the amount of gold that other countries were borrowing from the United States, leading to a policy that restricted the trade in 1971. Additionally, the economy was starting to see signs of stress: Inflation was rising, and the value of the dollar was falling. Citizens began to worry about their finances and the affordability of the comforts with which they had grown accustomed. The US support of Israel in 1973 led to a major oil crisis when the Arab members of the Organization of Petroleum Exporting Countries

(OPEC) enforced an embargo, and citizens experienced long gas lines at the pump for fear of running out of oil. The oil embargo did lead to increased attention to one of the first large-scale searches for alternative fuel sources, including solar, wind, and the Alaskan pipeline in 1973. This push was further exacerbated by President Carter's 1977 call for conservation and alternative fuels and Pennsylvania's Three-Mile Island nuclear plant troubles in 1979.[33]

With a continued push for civil rights, the Black Panthers formed in 1966 and stood in direct contradiction to the nonviolent messages preached by Martin Luther King Jr. Great change in racial relations was highlighted by the Miranda rights stemming from the historical ruling of *Miranda v. Arizona* and the Fifth Amendment in 1966 and by the appointment of Thurgood Marshall as the first African American Supreme Court justice in 1967.[34] During this era, immigration was prevalent, led by Mexico and Central America. The United States experienced "Hispanization," introducing both cultural and political consequences.

Women's rights issues were still important to this generation, as evidenced by the 1973 *Roe v. Wade* ruling that secured women's rights to their own bodies, even though this topic is still debated today, in 2020.[35] Women from this generation stood up to declare their rights, many of which resulted from the struggles of the baby boomers before them. Women also fought in court and secured equality in the workplace in 1972 with the passing of the Equal Employment Opportunity Act. A few years later, in 1978, the Pregnancy Discrimination Act was passed, establishing multiple laws that contributed to increased awareness and protections for women.[36]

As the civil rights movement continued to strengthen, the gay and lesbian movement was also gaining momentum and becoming more prominent. In 1969, a police raid in Greenwich Village, New York, led to riots and contributed to the formation of the LGBT rights movement, which momentarily included men and women; however, sexism within the movement caused women to branch out and continue to fight once again for their rights.[37] This movement took a big hit when San Francisco supervisor Harvey Milk, a vocal and openly gay politician, and Mayor George Moscone were both assassinated on November 28, 1978, by Dan White; their deaths prompted much more openness and activism, especially in the political arena.[38]

Poverty was also a concern for this generation. The war on poverty was an important focus, especially as the unemployment rate steadily rose to 9 percent in 1975, before declining to 5.6 percent in 1979, and then rising once again.[39]

As with previous generations, Generation X experienced substantial technological advancements. In 1969, NASA landed Neil Armstrong on the surface of the moon, who then uttered the famous words, "That's one small step for man, one giant leap for mankind."[40]

This event was miraculous for another reason, as well: the role that the media, specifically television, played in broadcasting it and bringing it to the lives of everyone with access. Television was securing its role as the primary mass medium of its time. Televisions were more affordable than ever, with expanded programming for increased entertainment. As a result, cable television became a terrific supplement to over-air broadcasting in the 1980s. Additionally, the world was introduced to the first home computers in 1977 with the user-friendly Apple II (Steve Wozniak's creation), changing the workplace and home forever.[41] Crucial foreign events, such as the 1980 Iranian hostage crisis led to the creation of the news program *Nightline*.[42] This generation also saw the results of increased health concerns, forcing advertisers to rein in their smoking ads.

SONY introduced the Betamax videocassette recorder in 1975, which was followed shortly by VHS tapes from Matsushita. The technology for laser discs then opened the door to the possibility of the compact disk and the Walkman, introduced in 1979, creating opportunities for portable music.

Clearly, the speed with which change happened in the world during Gen-Xers' childhoods enabled them to be the first generation to truly integrate and rely on technology and media, setting the tone for the next generation: millennials.

Millennials: 1981–1995

Millennials have many names: Gen-Me, the entitled generation, Generation Y, the net generation, Gen-Next, the digital generation, and the echo boom generation. This group of individuals has changed society at an unprecedented rate. They are nearly 80 million strong and known to be close to their parents and teachers.[43] Even when this generation leaves home for college, they tend to stay close and connected to their parents, normally via texting or social media.

Millennial clinginess can be attributed to how they were parented, and no other generation in history has exhibited this trait to the degree of millennials. Many parents of millennials are considered "snow-plow" parents, suggesting that they cleared the paths for their children's success by helping them every step of the way, even hindering independent thinking and action at times.[44] Because many of their parents are Gen-Xers, members of the latchkey generation who were taught to be independent at an early age, these millennial traits make sense.

Some assert that members of the millennial generation demonstrate the same ideals and principles associated with the workplace and classroom that were instituted by the baby boomers and even Generation X.[45] In contrast, others believe that they most mirror the traditionalist generation because they display a similar "I can do anything" attitude and are ready to change the world in positive ways.[46]

Millennials grew up with a heightened focus on education and recognized its value and necessity in becoming successful. Millennials were more widely exposed to diversity (e.g., gender, race, sexual orientation), and subsequently, many are more tolerant of differences within humans. In fact, 60 percent of millennials between the ages of eighteen and twenty-nine acknowledged being in a relationship with members of a different ethnicity, religion, or race, and the same percentage have multiracial friends.[47] This isn't surprising: Nearly one-third of millennials belong to a minority group.[48] This does not mean that all millennials are fully accepting of difference, but it does imply that many have witnessed or experienced diversity in their own lives or in the media and have learned to tolerate difference.

Technology could easily be considered most influential for millennials than for previous generations. Two-thirds of millennials used a computer before the age of five, and when their parents needed a break, many millennials were quieted at a young age with DVDs, TVs, smartphones, and iPads.[49] Many Gen-Xers and late baby boomers were raised on TV, and now there are more devices than ever to assist parents in calming their children or providing an alternate route of entertainment.

By far, the largest advances that the millennial generation has experienced include the advent of the Internet and the proceeding progression of the digital world. Computers, laptops, and iPads boosted technological confidence, while the Internet broke down countless barriers in allowing millennials to find and create their own online presence, often with their parents' blessing. However, because millennials are more tech-savvy than their baby boomer and Gen-X parents and are often left to their own devices, many find themselves in harm's way. A Pew Research Study found that more than eight in ten millennials sleep with a cell phone nightly so they can monitor texts, phone calls, e-mails, and what's happening online.[50]

Technology consumes every part of their lives, and this contributes to an innate ability to multitask, a trait many employers favor but that many parents and teachers are frustrated by. The knowledge and technological gaps between this generation and the previous generation continually has grown larger. Parents have had to evolve and become increasingly tech-savvy and media literate, and monitoring their children's technological lives was a good place to start.

Because of the prevalence of digital access, millennials have unprecedented access to world crises and global events.[51] Not unlike prior generations, they grew up during a time of notable global events that contributed to their beliefs, attitudes, and behaviors. The Columbine shootings in 1999; the tragic events of September 11, 2001; the downturn of the economy in 2008; widespread globalization; and even the introduction and mainstreaming of mobile phones, video games, and cable TV all contributed in some degree toward shaping the millennial generation.

Millennials have been lauded as the smartest generation ever.[52] Data tells us that raw IQ scores have increased by three points since World War II. As a result, more millennials are enrolled in undergraduate programs, and more are considering graduate programs than ever historically seen.[53] This also means that this generation is saddled with more school debt than any previous generation.

Millennials grew up in a time of transition for the economy and higher education. The office of Federal Student Aid reported that for 15.1 million borrowers ages twenty-five to thirty-four, there was $497.6 billion in outstanding student loan debt. Wesley Whistle, *Forbes* senior contributing author, said that "this translates to an average student debt of around $33,000 dollars for each borrower. For those ages 24 and younger, there was a cumulative loan balance of $124.6 billion for 8.1 million borrowers—an average of about $15,000 per borrower, though many of those borrowers may still be in school."[54] Combine this with the fact that millennials entered the workforce during a weak economy, and one can see why this generation is both entrepreneurial and conservative with spending money.

Thirty-one percent of millennials believe that they earn enough money to support the lifestyle they want.[55] Millennials fully believe that they could increase their earning potential. One way they accomplish this is to branch out and start their own businesses, often called a side hustle. Another is to play a meaningful role in the workplace. In the workplace, millennials expect to contribute positively and immediately take part in meaningful projects. What is important here is the word *meaningful*. Committed to producing high-quality results, this generation expects the same from others. They expect coworkers to be just as motivated as they are regarding success.

Having been set back by the recession and because success is a driver for many millennials, they entered the workforce with experience from several internships before ever leaving college. Their need to prove they are the smartest, most qualified, and best applicants for the position is a driving force behind their ambition.

Being happy in a job is one of the most important factors for millennials. This generation has switched careers or changed employers more regularly than previous generations.[56] They were often seen as job hoppers: Approximately 61 percent of millennials have found a new place of employment after only one year if they deemed their position to be detrimental to their careers, futures, or desires to achieve something better.[57]

Considered multitaskers, millennials juggle e-mails and multiple assignments and screen phone calls—all while trolling the Internet. When they feel caged, unhappy, or disinterested, millennials challenge their companies. Whereas baby boomers place a high degree of priority on their careers and live to work, millennials work to live and are most interested in developing a work-life balance that accommodates their families and personal lifestyles. They actively seek jobs that promote flexibility, telecommuting options, and the ability to work part time or leave the workforce temporarily when they become parents.[58]

Members of this generation want to contribute to the companies that they work for, but they are also self-reliant and independent. This means they are prepared to seek other options as often as necessary. Because millennials were taught to be self-confident and to fend for themselves, employers and coworkers sometimes interpret their independent nature as off-putting. The reality is that millennials were brought up receiving constant feedback and recognition from teachers, parents, and coaches, so if they have little or no communication and feedback from their supervisors, they feel lost and disconnected from the organization.[59] Millennials need to hear how they are progressing throughout the process, be rewarded for good work, and be praised publicly. The "look at me" generation likes to be noticed and acknowledged for jobs well done, no matter their age, race, gender, or sexual orientation.

In fact, millennials sometime want recognition for being unique or different from others, and this desire to accept or tolerate difference appears in many forms. Millennials are more ethnically and racially diverse than previous generations. They were also more highly educated and prone to settle down later in life. They are not of a single mind-set with respect to gender, partisanship, race, religious association, or sexual preferences. They were taught to "do their own thing" throughout their lives, so it should come as no surprise that they did not necessarily follow in their parents' footsteps.[60] For example, even if their parents consider themselves Republicans, this generation did not necessarily become Republican. When their parents frowned on interracial relationships, they embraced them. If they grew up Baptist, they might have tried Buddhism or Catholicism or even no form of organized religion at all.

This is not an act of rebellion; instead, millennials simply experienced and learned about difference in their real and mediated lives because more people challenged mainstream cultural norms in public arenas. The advent and adoption of the Internet provided quite the canvas for this generation to experience these varied opinions on a twenty-four-hour, global time scale. When baby boomers were fighting for women's, gay, and civil rights in the 1960s, magazines, music, and TV were the primary vehicles for expression and activism. In contrast, Twitter, Facebook, Snapchat, and Instagram make the news instantaneous for millennials, and privacy is no longer guaranteed in a world that is always *on* and where difference is often trending!

Millennials were taught to see the world from a global perspective. Gen-X parents, teachers, and mentors drilled into them the value of diversity. With this affinity for a globally diverse society, this generation is also more tolerant of lesbian, gay, bisexual, trans, queer, questioning, intersex, asexual, and pansexual (LGBTQQIAP) people than some members of previous generations. Gay rights only emerged after Stonewall in 1969, and many Gen-Xers were too young to participate in the gay movement until the late 1980s. However, many baby boomers led the way for equal rights until Gen-Xers came of age. Many Gen-Xers then raised their children with an open mind and heart toward a plethora of issues, LGBTQ+ among them.

For millennials, 2008 ushered in America's first African American president and along with it the next generation of voters. Nearly one-third of millennials entered the electorate to decisively support the election of Barack Obama. Furthermore, the support for President Obama from the younger generation crossed all ethnic groups. Obama won the votes of a majority of African American (95 percent), Latino (76 percent), and White (54 percent) young people, and having digital natives share his social media feeds may have made the difference.[61]

Additionally, many millennials were, and some still are, apathetic toward religion and the strict rules on premarital sex and marriage. They were raised during a time when the Catholic Church was under direct scrutiny for sexual abuse by priests around the world and while Islamic extremist groups led many global uprisings. These events made them generally less apt to develop a traditional bond to any specific religion; they are much more open-minded about investigating many religions. They are not anti-Christian, antireligion, or antimarriage, but they are, general speaking, simply not as interested in organized religion or being married, and many are self-identified atheists.

Individuals from this generation are not typically judgmental toward others' decisions or beliefs or whether their peers decide to marry. It is not that millennials don't want to get married; rather, many choose to wait until they are financially ready.[62] Because this generation values stability, they do not jump into marriage without thinking critically about the ramifications. Career ambitions and being financially stable were and remain important. When they marry, they want their relationships to last. To millennials, education and a steady income are paramount to having a healthy marriage; therefore, they often delay marriage until they feel that they can enter into the union successfully.

CHAPTER 1

INFLUENCING THE NEXT GENERATION: GENERATION Z

There is no doubt that differences between the generations exist. However, it is those differences that influence and build from one generation to the next, influencing who they become. In chapters 2 and 3, we set the context for and introduce Generation Z as the superhero generation. Utterly entrenched with fandom and fascination with these superbeings, this next generation exhibits many of the qualities of their favorite superheroes. And they may just save the world, too.

2

INTRODUCING THE SUPERHERO GENERATION

Characteristics and Importance

"Heroes are made by the path they choose, not the powers they are graced with."—Iron Man

The first decade of the twenty-first century fostered an atmosphere of fear, dating back to the ongoing struggles in the Middle East and highlighted by the attacks on the United States on September 11, 2001. As with other globally impactful historical events, 9/11 lives in infamy, with the Internet and other technological advances providing an open window to revisit those moments with poignant clarity with the touch of a button.

As worldwide tensions continue to reshape societies, both in the United States and abroad, justice and patriotism have become themes for many young people. Hollywood producers, filmmakers, and actors have ridden this wave of justice. Through books and film, the public has been introduced to role models who are reimagined and integrated into popular culture. Both DC Comics' and Marvel Comics' enterprises have had continuous success in bringing their superheroes to the big screens around the globe. Since 2000, twenty-three films have been produced for this genre, grossing billions of dollars.[1] Spinoffs and sequels, such as DC Comics' *Wonder Woman 1984* and *Birds of Prey* and Marvel Comics' *Black Widow* and *Dr. Strange in the*

Multiverse of Madness, appeal to those Gen-Zers, millennials, and Gen-Xers who may have witnessed or even experienced injustice in a complicated modern world.[2]

THE BIRTH OF THE SUPERHERO

The reemergence of today's superheroes parallels the late silent and early traditionalist generations' introduction to the same in mainstream culture. For instance, in 1936, just before the commencement of World War II and as Hitler was rising as a global power, Superman was introduced to the comic book world. Comics had been present in American culture since the late 1800s, but superheroes were a new phenomenon. Superman's interactions with Hitler were depicted on the cover of the first installment of the series and reflected the growing US presence in the global conflict. In fact, the superhero became a metaphor for the United States and its state of patriotism. It also became propaganda: Superman would point at the reader and request action in support of the ongoing war efforts. The mirroring of the real world within the popular culture world (or vice versa) continued through the 1950s with communism and the 1960s with civil rights, prominent issues in the United States.

The arrival of the first African American superhero occurred in the 1960s. In 1966, Stan Lee, creator and arguably the most well-known contributor to Marvel Comics, took a chance when he introduced an African American superhero, Black Panther, to the comic book community, largely in reflection of the growing cultural demands for civil rights and opportunities. Black Panther initially appeared on his own and was also paired with the Avengers and the Fantastic Four.

After the introduction of Black Panther, the comic book world and real-world events seemed to cross paths more regularly, helping set the precedent for other characters to gain a following—including a teenage Muslim female superhero (Ms. Marvel), an overweight superhero (Faith), a gay superhero (Green Lantern), and even more diverse characters. Everyday humans with technologically or biologically extraordinary powers—gifted through heritage, bloodline, or accident—have tackled real-world problems, and this story line continues even today.

INTRODUCING THE SUPERHERO GENERATION

Gen-Z has grown up with these superheroes at the forefront of society, exposing them at an early age to countless movies, comic books, and TV shows that follow the triumphs and tribulations of fallible beings. Marvel Studios' *Black Widow* and *The Falcon and the Winter Soldier*, DC Comics' *Birds of Prey* and *Stargirl*, and PS4's video game *Spider-Man* exemplify the persistent mainstream exposure that these characters continue to hold within society.[3] Many Gen-Zers identify with these superheroes and see in themselves potential superheroes ready to challenge injustice and change the world for the better.

Some superhero characteristics are more prominent in this generation than in prior generations, and we offer a short list to demonstrate the parallels to many Gen-Zers. We certainly are not proclaiming that Gen-Zers are god-like superheroes; rather, we acknowledge that technology has assisted them in creating and engaging the world in unique ways, so much so that they, too, can be perceived as "superhero-like." With a worldwide fascination with superheroes, it should come as no surprise that Gen-Zers mimic many of the characteristics found within the pages of the most popular hero-centric comic books.

Double Identity: Real World and Online World

In general, the backstories of many of our favorite superheroes indicate that these characters have either alter egos or double identities. From Clark Kent as Superman to Bruce Wayne as Batman, from Carol Danvers as Captain Marvel to Diana Prince as Wonder Woman, superheroes are known for keeping their superhero identities secret from as many people as possible while also engaging in everyday interactions as students (Ms. Marvel) and CEOs (Iron Man).

Like many of these superheroes, Gen-Zers also have two distinct identities: one online and the other in the real world. For them, their online identity may consist of actually more than one identity, as each social media platform demands a different identity. For example, in video games, avatars are built or bought with real money or online credits earned through play. On social media, our real-world identities are often masked by our

Instagram, Snapchat, and Twitter photos and handles. People can create new identities in online worlds via social media and gaming and never have to reveal their real-world identities, which of course has various advantages and disadvantages.

One distinct advantage of an online identity is being able to speak and present ourselves as we see fit. This encourages us to use our voices, take creative risks, and expand our networks, all of which can lead to positive self-esteem, increased confidence, and even unplanned professional op-portunities. However, one distinct disadvantage of these masked identities is that we can also be followed or liked by people with whom we don't want to be associated. Some risk-taking may backfire and lead to professional discrediting, online embarrassment, or even online harassment. Regardless, maintaining and building more than one "self" for a variety of publics can be exhausting, time consuming, and stressful. Being online means being "on" or present for others throughout the day, maybe even 24/7. This identity maintenance may make it difficult for Gen-Zers who have known no other world. That said, these multiple identities also provide space and voice to fight for many causes.

The Fight for "Just" Causes

Superheroes are known to position themselves on the side of good, not evil. They make choices based on their individual, utilitarian sense of morality or rightness, even if that means taking another's life in the process. We seem-ingly encounter the greater-good utilitarian philosophy most often in the comic book world: Utilitarianism "holds that an action is *right* if it leads to the *most happiness* for the *greatest number* of people" and happiness equals the "maximization of pleasure and the minimization of pain."[4]

The causes these superheroes support can be personal, such as the villain has killed their parents or other loved ones, as in the backstory for Batman, Spider-Man, and Superman; or they can be environmental or global, such as a villain wanting to take over the world or poison a city through its water or food source. However, the end game (no pun intended) is happiness for the greatest number, even if the greatest number equates only two identities. Nonetheless, superheroes immediately stand up for justice as they, their or-ganizations, or cultural norms see fit. They may encounter ethical dilemmas in making these choices, but they seem to persevere on the side of supposed personalized justice.

By definition, superheroes are meant to save the day. With an arch nemesis seemingly around every corner, they are fully equipped with unique superpowers to overcome any challenge. With that in mind, Gen-Z is standing up for many of the same ideals that superheroes fight for: systematic and transformative social change. Such movements as the Women's March, Me Too, Time's Up, Black Lives Matter, and Gun Control Now not only spurred action on the social sphere, but they also illustrated how social media provides a platform for the masses to amplify their voices and, in turn, work together to carry forth the message of a movement. This generation is not afraid to stand up for their values. They are marching. They are assembling. They are organizing. They are speaking out.

Second Job: They Can't Just Be Superheroes

In the history of comic book superheroes, their independence has connections, financial or otherwise, to larger organizations or networks, and sometimes their careers reflect and inform their choices. For example, Superman saves people but in doing so brings much attention to himself as a superhero and to the *Daily Planet* newspaper as his employer. Clark Kent, a *Daily Planet* reporter, doesn't always get "kudos" for bringing down a villain, but without Kent embracing his alter ego, the newspaper wouldn't be able to publish some of its stories or sell as many newspapers. The relationships between Superman, Clark Kent, and reporters like Lois Lane are very much symbiotic, in that Superman needs the Clark Kent cover, and the newspaper needs Superman to sell newspapers (greater good).

However, Superman is not the only superhero associated with larger organizations. In Marvel Comics, S.H.I.E.L.D. is the overarching network for which the Avengers work: "These days, S.H.I.E.L.D. stands for 'Strategic Homeland Intervention, Enforcement and Logistics Division,' but it previously also stood for 'Strategic Hazard Intervention Espionage Logistics Directorate' and, originally, 'Supreme Headquarters, International Espionage, Law-Enforcement Division.'"[5] The Avengers include superheroes working as individuals or as a team, made up of characters like Black Panther, Black Widow, Captain America, Captain Marvel, and many others. The Avengers,

X-Men, and Fantastic Four are also teams of superheroes connected to some larger organization or governing body who join forces in the comics universe to take down a villain. They put their individual, real-world alter egos aside for a short time with hopes of returning to them and maintaining their cover or anonymity. In a sense, the emergence of superheroes throughout history mirrored the baby boom generation's "live to work" mentality, imagined as superheroes, but also the "work to live" mantra of Generation X, representing their alter egos or real-world working selves. The fact that Gen-Zers have superpowers is not always innate or readily recognizable until adversity of some sort emerges.

EXTRAORDINARY POWER OR ABILITY: HOW DO THEY GET THESE SUPERPOWERS?

Superheroes vary in their superpowers and abilities. They are either born with special powers (e.g., Superman, Wonder Woman); gain their powers as a result of a science experiment gone wrong (e.g., Hulk, Spider-Man, X-Men), or are technologically empowered by specially engineered suits or accessories (e.g., Iron Man, Ant Man, Captain America, Captain Marvel). Regardless of how they obtained their superpower or ability, each is distinctly different from the others, preserving the individuality of the superhero. A superhero is distinct from other superheroes in their powers or abilities, but they are also alike in their overall views of the world and the adversities they face.

Superheroes Face Adversity

The fact that a character can be defined as a superhero indicates that they are already positioned as superior to humans based on their extraordinary powers or abilities and are therefore often depicted as dangers to society. Police, government, or other ruling bodies perceive their behaviors as rogue or vigilante-like, thus they are threats to cultural norms and laws. Bruce Wayne's Batman is one clear example of this. Batman may capture the Joker and other villains, but he, too, must escape the law or be jailed, despite his good deeds. While much of the adversity they face as superheroes is based in xenophobia (fear of the unknown or strange), many of their alter egos face adversity, as well. This can be seen through their social awkwardness (e.g., Clark Kent); extreme beauty or handsomeness (e.g., Diana Prince); occupational success (e.g., Dr. Strange); obesity (e.g., Faith); or religion (Ms. Marvel). The real world is not a place these individuals can thrive as themselves, so they each have an alternate superhero world to thrive in. These characters need both identities to feel like they are part of something bigger than they are, ultimately increasing their potential for fallibility in both worlds. Gen-Zers thrive in much the same way. They need their online personas to complete their identities.

Superheroes Are Fallible

Because superheroes need alter egos to provide a sense of anonymity, they can be considered fallible. In fact, one of the more appealing superhero characteristics is the ability to fail. As each of these characters is human in some respect, whether biologically, emotionally, or culturally, readers and viewers alike embrace their fallibility in much the same way many cultures accept humanness as a fallibility.

This term, *fallibility*, is used to describe mistakes that are related to physical, mental, cognitive, or emotional weaknesses and that can counteract one's perceived superordinary abilities. Death may be a consequence for real humans, but for many superheroes, death is not the end game. Instead, losing their identity, self-esteem, or even power can affect the greater good's realization of a successful outcome. However, being unmasked or recognized by the public is a superhero's biggest fallibility because it eliminates the identities in both the real and superhero worlds. In a sense, being revealed means simultaneously dismantling two identities. The desire for infallibility is what superheroes project through their actions, but the reality is that one mistake can destroy many lives, including their own.

Superheroes Are Independent

During the course of saving lives and foiling evil plans, superheroes tend to prefer to go about their business alone. It is their own perceived infallibility that provides confidence for doing good deeds for the masses, and they are generally capable of pulling off these feats while solo. This is not to say that they do not work with teams; they often recognize that a network is far more capable or necessary to be successful.

GEN-Z ASSUMING THE SUPERHERO ROLE

The characteristics described in this chapter fit most superheroes. Sometimes, they, too, can go rogue and must be contained or managed by others. But that change from superhero to villain is often influenced by their human fallibility or by some environmental influence that severely alters their superhero mind-set. Similar to previous generations, Gen-Zers want to change the world. But just like superheroes, they may not be fully equipped for making change happen. Their desire and willingness are often short-sighted, as they are still developing their identities. However, many of their strongest characteristics reflect the superhero mind-set. In the next chapter, we explore these superhero characteristics, supporting the notion that Gen-Z truly is the superhero generation.

3

GENERATION Z

Superheroes Rise!

*"If anyone found out what we truly are and what we pos-
sess, it could destroy the world. It is my duty to protect
it."—Black Panther*

Superheroes lead complex lives and are tested to maintain the balance
between two distinct identities: real-world and superhero. This chapter explains how Gen-Z exhibits the superhero characteristics previously
discussed. We know that Gen-Zers are not *actual* superheroes. However,
superhero characteristics are prevalent in Gen-Z's "digiverse" experiences.
Although the term *digiverse* describes the digitalization of Cyrus Borg in the
fantasy series *Ninjago*, we primarily use it to describe the world that these
digital natives have lived in from birth[1]:

> The iPhone launched in 2007 when the oldest Gen-Zers were 10. By the time
> they were in their teens, the primary means by which young Americans con-
> nected with the web was through mobile devices, WiFi and high-bandwidth
> cellular service. Social media, constant connectivity, and on-demand enter-
> tainment and communication are innovations Millennials adapted to as they
> came of age. For those born after 1996, these are largely assumed.[2]

In fact, "Over half of Gen Z uses their smartphone five or more hours per day. But of these, 26% use ten or more hours each day!"[3] With this increased use of technology, *digiverse* refers to the digital world as we know it in 2020. It also explains the role that double identities play for these digital natives—much like superheroes.

DOUBLE IDENTITY: REAL WORLD AND ONLINE WORLD

Just as superheroes live double lives, so do Gen-Zers. They live and cultivate identities in both the real world and online communities. Much like previous generations, Gen-Z must decide how or if to present their real-world lives in online worlds.

Business professionals thought of this early on; LinkedIn, a professionally oriented social media platform, emerged as the most viable option for business professionals to share advice, search and post jobs, post résumés, and connect with others in their fields. LinkedIn differs from other social media platforms because the focus is on one's career rather than being predominantly socially oriented.

As Gen-Z matures, they have migrated away from Facebook, where Gen-Xers and boomers tend to hang out and where privacy is harder to control, to other social media platforms, such as Instagram, Snapchat, TikTok, and Twitter, where privacy settings are easier to control and one's persona can be more readily maintained. Personas can change from platform to platform through bios, handles, and photos. In the digiverse, multiple identities are standard. Because the presence of different identities is possible and expected, social media has made it easier for Gen-Zers to connect with a multitude of people from all over the world.

Managing Multiple Identities

With an increased availability of and access to technological platforms and devices, Gen-Zers feel the pressure to be connected to others at a moment's notice. Katie Steinmetz notes, "There's so much pressure on young people, who are still forming their identities, to present this crystallized, idealized identity online."[4] Data supports the claim that Gen-Zers are spending ten waking hours a day connected to their devices, particularly their smart-phones. They aren't just connecting with their latest online friend, seeking out what their favorite celebrity is doing, or catching up on the latest news in their feeds; they are also managing their identities.

Gen-Zers are branding themselves from the time they first begin posting on social media platforms. For some, this starts early, with parents posting not only their prebirth ultrasounds but also countless childhood moments for friends to see. Gen-Zers face increasing pressure to be liked on social media and must determine early on how they would like to present themselves on these social media platforms. While superheroes manage two identities for audiences, ironically, Gen-Zers may be simultaneously managing three or more personas, depending on their social media presence.

However, an even thinner line exists these days between what details should be kept private and what can be shared publicly. We all know some-one who has posted a sonogram of an unborn child, set up an account for their toddler, or shared way too much information about their personal intimacies on Facebook, Instagram, and TikTok. The line between public and private lives become more blurred each day with each post. Users pro-duce more than 1.2 million pieces of shared data daily through social media platforms. Every minute, 100 million text or in-app messages are sent, nearly 70 million videos and photos are uploaded to Instagram, and 4.3 million YouTube videos are accessed.[5] So while Gen-Zers admit that privacy is im-portant, not many are willing to give up the conveniences that come with a loss of privacy. For example, many Gen-Zers use Wi-Fi to conduct personal banking business—as it is convenient to do—but they also know they are putting their identities at risk; convenience often outvies privacy. However, beyond privacy and managing identities, Gen-Zers, like their superhero pre-decessors, fight for "just causes."

PRINCIPLED SUPERHEROES

Just as their comic book superheroes have done, younger Gen-Zers also seem more willing than previous generations did to stand up and fight for justice. These individuals are socially conscious and demand equality, even from their employers.[6] The phrase *stand up* is an interesting one because hashtag activism doesn't require the activist to physically stand up (or even sit up) to participate. Hashtag activism involves presenting one's beliefs and values via shared online tools in support of a cause and grows when people elect to follow and use the same hashtag (#) on social media. Activism, in this case, begins virtually and then extends into the real world. While many millennials engaged in hashtag or virtual activism, others avoided in-person protests, marches, and events. However, Gen-Zers seem to be more willing to actually stand up and march or sit-in or die-in for their causes, especially concerning gun violence, environmental issues, and civil rights—just as many late baby boomers and early Gen-Xers have done in the past.[7] This is because their parents taught them from a young age that they have a voice and what they *say* and *do* matters.

Take, for example, the group of students who rallied around gun control legislation after the school shooting at Marjory Stoneman Douglas High School in 2018. While organizing has been savvy and effective for garnering attention, resulting gun control policies are still a goal, not a reality, as an additional 300 people have died and "more than 1,300 [have been] wounded" since this tragedy.[8] Despite slow legislative changes, Gen-Zers continue to advocate, knowing that change is slow and will happen over time. Their relentlessness is part of their grit. In fact, social justice is so important that even when looking for love, they proudly tout their causes in their bios.

When seeking a hookup, or a date, Gen-Z focuses on the importance of social justice in their lives. "According to Tinder's 2019 Year In Swipe report, users between the ages of 18 and 24, who now make up the majority of the dating and hookup app's users, were 66% more likely than Millennials to mention issues like climate change, gun control, or social justice in their bios."[9]

Activism isn't a fad or passing phase for many Gen-Zers; it is part of their identity. Organizations that want to attract and retain Gen-Zers will need to take this into consideration. For example, Levi Strauss and Co. announced that it launched a series of initiatives to support organizations and people in favor of gun control.[10] Ben and Jerry's boldly embraces the brand's social activism and purposeful DNA. They are unapologetic and bold in their approach to issues they care about. Patagonia is similar. They've always been a politically driven brand. They publicly endorse politicians and are not afraid to make their stance known. In the 2020 presidential election, they gained buzz on social media after people noticed "Vote the assholes out" hidden on some of their tags.[11] Such bold moves will preferentially identify and help retain Gen-Zers in the workplace. Previous generations of workers may have looked for a better work-life balance or extra vacation days, but this generation wants these in addition to working for a company with a conscience.

Environmentalists

Greta Thunberg, *Time* magazine's 2019 person of the year, is one clear example of this generation's passion for the environment.[12] She left her school and home in Stockholm, Sweden, at the age of sixteen to fight for changes in global climate policies, both domestically and abroad. Her commitment to saving the earth has placed her squarely in the global spotlight. Thunberg is not fighting to save the planet for fame; rather, her stance arises from saving others and the world. She is putting the greater good ahead of all else, just as a superhero would.

While Greta may be the most recognizable name behind climate change, there are other Gen-Zers who are equally important in the fight for the environment closer to home: Isra Hirsi, daughter of US representative Ilhan Omar, has been a longtime social justice activist and now climate activist; Autumn Peltier has been an activist since the age of eight, beginning with a toxic water warning and emerging as a teenager fighting for water conservation and indigenous water rights and against pipeline projects; and Mari Copeny (a.k.a., "Little Miss Flint"), who, at the age of eight, wrote a letter to then-president Barack Obama about the Flint water crisis and continues to support water issues through her #WednesdaysForWater and more.[13]

Just as superheroes find moral, personal, or ethical reasons to fight supervillains, Gen-Zers fight, too. They might not engage in the physical confrontations or fisticuffs that superheroes typically do, but they often get involved by being physically present or vocal regarding relevant issues, leveraging social media, videos, and live events and marches. When they align themselves with causes on social media, they do so by joining groups, chatting, or following hashtags, either in online forums or with their school peers.

Women's Rights

One of the most prominent hashtags over the last couple of decades is #MeToo—gaining mainstream attention in 2017 when allegations against Hollywood film producer Harvey Weinstein surfaced. The hashtag was started by Taran Burke, a sexual harassment survivor and activist. It went viral when Alyssa Milano tweeted, "If all the women who have been sexually harassed or assaulted wrote 'Me too' as a status, we might give people a sense of the magnitude of the problem."[14] Other famous actors, including Uma Thurman, Ashley Judd, Gwyneth Paltrow, and Jennifer Lawrence, followed suit. Women of all ages who have experienced sexual harassment, assault, or rape have used the hashtag in solidarity. Seeing friends, relatives, and strangers using the hashtag has reminded people that they aren't alone and that these issues are still prominent in women's lives.

Women not only rallied around the hashtag, but they also rallied in Washington, DC, and all over the world to stand up to continued injustices. Other prominent people accused of sexual harassment, assault, or misconduct revealed during the Me Too movement include Bill Cosby, Jeffrey Epstein, Matt Lauer, Charlie Rose, Cristiano Ronaldo, and, US president Donald J. Trump.[15] The Me Too movement will have cultural implications and repercussions for years to come, and Gen-Zers, both celebrities and laypeople, will lead the way.

Beyond the Me Too movement, Gen-Zers are championing other aspects of women's rights, such as basic human, biological, and reproductive rights. Malala Yousafzai, a Pakistani girl, was shot in 2012 while trying to assist girls in receiving a proper education. Nadya Okamoto, founder and executive director of PERIOD, was appalled by the tampon tax and now makes feminine hygiene products accessible and affordable around the globe. Virginia teen Sejal Makheja started a job training project for those living in poverty when she was fourteen. These are just a few women creating transformative changes.[16]

Human Rights and Social Justice

Gen-Zers are also passionate about human rights. In the United States, there is a renewed focus on immigration and associated struggles. The similarities to the internment of Japanese Americans in the United States during World War II is uncanny. Images of forced incarceration and relocation of immigrants are flooding social and mainstream media. During their Superbowl LIV performance of "Let's Get Loud," Jennifer Lopez (J.Lo) and Shakira displayed young performers, including Lopez's eleven-year-old daughter, Emme, in birdcage-like set pieces across the stage, a call for immigration reform here in the United States.[17] Emme, a Gen-Zer, raised concerns about immigration through her performance.

LGBTQ+ (lesbian, gay, bisexual, trans, queer, questioning, intersex, asexual, and pansexual) rights are also important to Gen-Z. Much like millennials, most Gen-Zers acknowledge the importance of gender fluidity—not presenting one male or female cultural identity—including the rights of those who identify as lesbian, gay, bisexual, and more. In the United Kingdom, students protested the firing of two teachers, one gay and the other lesbian, while during a separate political rally in the United States, a nine-year-old boy asked Pete Buttigieg, an openly gay Democratic candidate for president, to assist him in coming out. Zachary Ro wrote in a question, chosen via fishbowl during the presidential hopefuls Saturday rally: "Would you help me tell the world I'm gay, too? I want to be brave like you."[18] Clearly, Gen-Z is passionate about these rights and their individual identities.

Caring for others who have less than most seems to be quite a common theme for Gen-Z. Members of this generation use their technological prowess to raise money for charitable causes that affect them on a basic human level. Fighting poverty, genocide, and human trafficking seem second nature to many Gen-Zers. Their fights may seem like uphill battles, but many are conditioned from a young age, perhaps provoked by global and regional crises, to succeed and make the world a better place. The causes they fight are the supervillains of their time.

EXTRAORDINARY POWER OR ABILITY: WIRED TO THE DIGIVERSE

So, what exactly are Gen-Z's extraordinary powers or abilities? As far as we know, no Gen-Zer has been granted superhero powers via a science experiment gone awry or through familial bloodlines. However, what we do know is that this generation is the first to be described as "digital natives": those born into an already-existing digital world.[19] While these individuals may not have been cognizant of the digiverse at birth or even in their formative years, this generation will never truly know a world without digital technologies. They recreate, learn, and work in a digital world, which will ultimately continue to influence their home, educational, and work environments.

ENTREPRENEURIAL SPIRIT

Millennials were heralded for their ability to think outside the box as they entered the workplace, and their entrepreneurial spirit was noteworthy. While many millennials were exemplary role models for this next generation, Gen-Zers appear to embrace their entrepreneurial spirit at an even earlier age.[20] For example, there are young children who have their own YouTube channels and make millions of dollars in their early elementary school years.

In Albany, New York, seven-year-old Kennedy O'Neal created a music video called "PiggyBank" to assist others in saving money.[21] While her parents may have encouraged her to start saving her money early, they also noticed her ability to discuss this financial principal using layperson's terms, so much so that even a five-year-old would be able to understand the importance of saving money. There is also Ryan Kaji, who at the age of eight earned $26 million in 2019 by "conducting science experiments and branched out beyond YouTube with a line of more than 100 toys, clothing items and more, a show on Nickelodeon and a deal with Hulu."[22]

Branding themselves on various social media platforms, Gen-Zers must balance their identities on an active, ongoing basis from an early age so as not to lose likes, friends, followers, or even a livelihood. In a sense, this ability is extraordinary, as no other generation has had to do this from early childhood. While it may place undue pressure on Gen-Zers to always be "present" for others, it is also amazing just how quickly and fluidly they can do so. Technology allows this generation to secure a superpower that generations before them have never been able to do at such an early age.

Marketing Dollars

Consider this, as well: While TV ushered in the idea of children as viable consumers, the Internet and widespread access to social media have taken them to an even higher level. The cultural gap in technology and access for citizens has nearly disappeared. Couple this with the noticeably soft regulation of the Internet, and you have a place where advertisers and marketers can have a field day connecting with this multibillion-dollar market. Organizations seek and hire brand influencers, looking for just the right person across social media platforms to tout their products or services and earn followers—which can lead to more profit.

FALLIBILITY

As discussed earlier, superheroes may believe they are infallible, but fallibility is part of their overall identities. Their humanness opens them up to mistakes, wherein their extraordinary powers or abilities may become ineffective or absent. The same is true for Gen-Zers. They, too, are human, and their fallibility is tied to their dependence on technology in the digiverse.

Fear of Missing Out (FOMO)

Why do Gen-Zers and others stay so connected to their smartphones, tablets, and wearable devices? Just like their millennial predecessors, they also suffer from FOMO—the fear of missing out. While earlier generations consumed their news using electronic and broadcast media, such as TV and radio, Gen-Z receives their news, notifications, ads, and photos instantaneously, 24/7—much faster than any of the generations that preceded them.

Because breaking news and world events are essentially available on demand, much of what members of this generation fear missing out on is usually a text, direct message, or post on their social media accounts. News outlets feed this fear as they seek to break the story first, even if accuracy is compromised. For example, TMZ, a celebrity news outlet focusing on a thirty-mile radius of Los Angeles, California, broke the news about the helicopter crash that claimed the life of NBA legend Kobe Bryant before even verifying the report from a credible source.[23] In fact, many social media users shared that news before they had confirmation from other, noncelebrity news sources. At the same time, they also expressed their concern and hoped the news was inaccurate, as it had been in the past.[24] TMZ's news approach emphasizes that it is better to be first than to consider the consequences, even if inaccuracy is the result. While their reporting may have been accurate, questions were raised about the ethical implications of announcing it *before* his family had been notified. TMZ is still working hard to be viewed as a credible news source—even more so with Gen-Zers, who aren't as media literate as their generational counterparts.

FOMO is not only limited to just worldwide breaking news, but it also extends to the friends and families of Gen-Zers and their personal networks. Gen-Xers and those generations that came before them didn't have the connectivity to others with the immediacy of today's technology. Passing a note in the classroom may have been the quickest way to tell a friend something during class. That other person had to be in the room to receive the message at that time, with a chain of other accomplices helping to pass it along. A phone call to a parent while on school property meant finding a pay phone and some spare change and hoping that the parent was at work or at home for you to reach them. Now, texts can be sent from one person to another with little effort and thought, whether they are sent to friends or family; no loose change needs to be found for a phone call.

But what are Gen-Zers *really* missing if they don't check their messages? Most of the time, Gen-Z is missing out on everyday chatter and happenings. However, having grown up with mass killings on school property and regularly scheduled lock-down drills, that one moment of connectivity may be the difference between life and death. Yes, Gen-Zers may spend much of their downtime flitting through social media sites and texts, but they would rather be connected just *in case* something happens and they need to know right now. After all, they grew up during a time when their safety is at risk, even at school.

The FOMO experience also creates social anxiety for those who can't afford to go to a concert, event, or social gathering. Self-esteem is lowered when those who are online don't believe they measure up to their peers' online personas displayed via selfies and photos with fun hashtags. How often do you see friends and family on a vacation, at an event, or even at a restaurant with pictures of their meals—often referred to as "food porn"—and think to yourself, "I wish I could be doing that" or "How can they afford that"? This jealousy is also reflected in the fear of living off-line, or FOLO.

Fear of Living Off-Line (FOLO)

Remember: Most of Gen-Z has never known a world that wasn't digitally accessible at a moment's notice. If they turn a phone off while in class or at work, then their anxiety often increases, as does the stress that they experience. The what-if is the most important part of being connected. *What if* you lost your wallet and needed a ride? *What if* your friend needs a ride to the doctor? *What if* there is a shooter on school grounds? *What if* another attack happens on US soil? All the potential what-ifs consume people's thinking such that they can't manage the stress and anxiety that comes from *not* having their smartphones with them. Losing a smartphone is equivalent to losing a limb for many Gen-Zers. When they don't have their smartphones, they can experience phantom buzzing, much like those who have lost a limb may still feel like the limb is there.

Not only do Gen-Zers experience FOLO, but those around them do, as well. Millennials, Gen-Xers, and some baby boomers may even experience FOLO in today's world. It is often impossible to go off the grid because wireless networks can be found for free in so many places. Someone may have to intentionally seek out a tech-free spot with no access to Wi-Fi, which is becoming increasingly difficult to do. Then, if they do live off-line for even a few hours, their loved ones and colleagues worry incessantly about them. They wonder about their absence, either in person or through personal text, e-mail, or social media.

Living in the digiverse changed our experiences of going to concerts, social gatherings, and other cultural events. There is now an unwritten social expectation: If you attend an event that others can't attend, then you will post pictures or video during the event. And others take part by viewing the photos and video, even if it means they are not actually experiencing it through their own eyes. This social expectation exists even for those who are physically with you at the event. Many artists have become frustrated with the use of smartphone videos during their events and have requested that their fans turn them off and just enjoy the show in person; after all, they paid good money to be present in person.

Selfies are another phenomenon resulting from FOLO. How many times have we engaged in or witnessed the awkward selfie pose, even if it puts us or others in danger? We take selfies not so much to save for later and put in a photo album but to post *now* so others can see who we are with and what we are doing; our personal brand demands constant updates so others can stay in the know—we feed their FOMO. The stress and anxiety brought on by FOMO and FOLO causes mental health and well-being challenges.

Mental Health Challenges: Stigma Schmigma

In generations prior to millennials, little, if any, public attention was given to psychiatric or psychological disorders. Those experiencing these disorders in mild forms were often dismissed or ignored, while those with more extreme disorders were hospitalized, which stigmatized and followed those people throughout their entire lives. Prior to the *Diagnostic and Statistical Manual* (DSM) removing homosexuality as a disease, many gay people were considered "outside the cultural norm," hospitalized, and treated with shock therapy to convert them to heterosexuality. In 1973, the DSM removed that label, and suddenly homosexuality was "cured."[25] But the physical, emotional, and cultural scars remained.

Discussions of someone's mental health was considered taboo, so sufferers often went untreated or unrecognized by larger society. To admit a weakness in one's own mental health was unwelcome, and many people were often denied a call for help. Enter millennials, who began to openly discuss their mental health in a variety of media outlets and on social media platforms. The Internet provided opportunities for many to reach out to others having similar experiences. With technology at our fingertips, many began to hear from and see others share their personal challenges, lessening the loneliness often associated with mental illness.

Anxiety, Depression, Stress, and Lack of Quality Sleep

While public speaking is still the top fear-inducing and anxiety-ridden activity for many people, others have noticed that social anxiety has become increasingly prevalent among those who spend much time glued to their technologies. Psychiatrists began to use the term *nomophobia* to refer to FOMO and FOLO. Although not included in the most recent update of the DSM (V), it has been proposed for acceptance based on definitions included in previous editions.

Nomophobia is not just a simple fear but a deeper, ingrained fear of being without one's mobile phone, which then leads to stress. Dr. Nicola Davies, prolific senior medical writer in health psychology, notes,

> Often associated with separation anxiety, nomophobia comes with a set of identifiable symptoms: increased heart rate and blood pressure, shortness of breath, anxiety, nausea, trembling, dizziness, depression, discomfort, fear, and panic. However, there is debate within the medical community on its classification; is it a phobia, anxiety disorder, lifestyle disorder, or addiction?[26]

Migraines, weight loss or gain, fatigue, and other symptoms are now associated with many Gen-Zers. Poor spatial skills, inability to navigate streets without GPS, and increased risk of obesity are also disconcerting.[27] Additionally, the blue light of a tablet or cellphone has intensified sleep deprivation for millennials, and Gen Z is currently the embodiment of a sleep-deprived generation. While researchers recognize that teens require anywhere from eight to ten hours of sleep a night to be truly functional (barring any other intrusions or disabilities), about 85 percent of Gen-Zers report that they do not achieve this minimum on a daily basis, with one in five teens getting fewer than five hours of quality sleep each night.[28] Teens often pride themselves on what little sleep they do get and compliment themselves for performing well each day. However, there are many side effects to repeated sleep deprivation, including but not limited to slower response times and lower grades. Certainly, the concern is real, and the discussion, important.

Emotional Consequences

In addition to the physical consequences associated with anxiety, depression, stress, and sleep deprivation, emotional consequences emerge, as well. One of the key indicators of workplace and relational success is attributed to an individual's level of emotional intelligence. What may be easy for some, emotional intelligence can often be quite difficult for others. Research suggests that females are more often in tune with emotions, while men experience more difficulty because they are more task-oriented than relational-oriented.[29] Daniel Goleman, an American psychologist and emotional intelligence advocate, says, "Emotional intelligence or EI is the ability to understand and manage your own emotions, and those of the people around you. People with a high degree of emotional intelligence know what they're feeling, what their emotions mean, and how these emotions can affect other people."[30] Emotional intelligence requires deeper attention to details than many of us are ready to endure. Just ask a college teacher who has been approached by a student about missing class, and you will hear stories about the lack of students' emotional intelligence.

INDEPENDENT: SORT OF

The last superhero characteristic that is important to cover, independence, turns out to be a bit more obscure. Many Gen-Zers tend to be quite confident in their abilities yet require ongoing feedback and direction in school, at home, and in the workplace. For example, if their navigation system is down, many Gen-Zers, and even some millennials, may not actually reach their destination because they don't know how to read a printed map. Technology, parents, and schools have lessened the ability of Gen-Zers to leverage this basic life skill. In fact, much like their millennial counterparts, many of their parents are snow-plow parents.[31] These parents not only guide their children to make good decisions, but they also often are responsible for the outcomes—good or bad. Unlike late Gen-Xers, who may have had helicopter parents who hovered and guided but didn't actually clear the way, Gen-Zers' parents are often the ones questioning, calling, and visiting schools, workplaces, and more to ensure their children succeed and obstacles are removed. All this coddling has earned them the nickname "cream puff generation."[32]

Parents typically want their children to succeed, but they don't often teach them to manage failure or overcome obstacles. From infancy, if a Gen-zer was upset or bored, they were often handed a technological device to occupy that brief moment of downtime rather than allowing them to experience boredom and contend with it in the moment. Parents race into action so as not to cause a public scene when children have tantrums. It's as if boredom or frustration can be detrimental to their psyches. Many Gen-Zers really don't know how to fill their free time, manage their frustrations, or overcome obstacles other than through social media. "Usage habits continue to increase, with a quarter checking their phones 30 times an hour and their smartphones every three minutes."[33] When they feel bored, they look externally to others to fill their time. When they are in class, they look to be entertained by others, either the teacher or their peers—but without a smartphone nearby their attention span is limited. Gen-Zers no longer write out their class notes when learning; rather, they prefer a laptop or tablet to take notes.

However, let's not be fooled: They also use their learning time to keep close tabs on their social media accounts, texts, and videos! They're anxious, stressed, and very distracted. This perceived lack of life skills doesn't prepare them to manage these experiences, so a lot of hand-holding is often required.[34] Within the workplace, this will be one of the biggest and most frustrating challenges for managers and coworkers. The necessity to explain and clarify tasks will try the patience of their peers and higher-ups. Their independence seemingly is more closely aligned as a dependence on others, especially in the online world. It would behoove parents, employers, and educators to encourage Gen-Zers to take risks, fail, and then manage the outcomes rather than getting the snowplow out and doing it for them. Hand-holding requires both parties to be present and involved in the outcome, but it only takes one person to snowplow, and parents need to sit back a bit so that their children can press onward and achieve independence.

Ultimately, every generation seeks to achieve its own independence. But prior to the digiverse, there were distinct ways to avoid dependence on others. For example, in the 1980s, if you didn't want to engage with someone, then you avoided the physical spaces they would occupy. If they tried to reach you by telephone, you could ignore the ringing and go about your business. You went about your days without getting a message from siblings, coworkers, friends, and family, and you didn't experience FOMO in the same way Gen-Zers do today. In fact, FOLO could not have even been conceivable at that time because the world wasn't online and the digiverse was merely a fantasy.

As you can see, Gen-Z exhibits the superhero characteristics that we've already touched on. No wonder stress and anxiety often run rampant among this generation! Teaching life skills to all generations certainly prepares them better for success—and failure.

MASKED CRUSADERS

Generation Z in Action

4

DOUBLE IDENTITY

Empowerment, Entrepreneurship, Independence

"It's not who I am underneath, but what I do, that defines me."—Batman

Historically speaking, each generation holds a series of stereotypes about the others that negatively affects both workplace relationships and productivity. As of 2020, Gen-Z accounts for roughly 20 percent of the overall population, and by 2030, Gen-Z will be responsible for nearly 30 percent of the broader workforce.[1] Currently, organizations are often employing four generations, comprised of baby boomers, Gen-Xers, millennials, and the oldest Gen-Zers (aged 23 or so), with very different work ethics, values, and expectations. On rare occasions, a fifth generation, Traditionalists, may also be employed by the same organization. These cross-generational workforces make one thing clear: Intergenerational communication in the workplace will continue to be a challenge for any organization, with technology making it both more complex and immediate. The Internet, e-mail, social media platforms, and virtual meetings have changed the rules for workplace communication and how we create and maintain workplace relationships.

SUPERHEROES OR VILLAINS?

As you may be able to conclude by now, members of Generation Z are often simultaneously perceived as *both* superheroes and villains, based on their personal circumstances and how they relate to others. Their superhero characteristics can most certainly benefit the workplace, but they also create a multitude of challenges.

SUPERHERO CHARACTERISTICS THAT BENEFIT THE WORKPLACE

Double Identities

In US comic book culture, superheroes live under the guise of dual identities, one that they share publicly and one that is hidden from the world. All superheroes have a private life completely disconnected from their public heroic acts. For example, Wonder Woman's backstory, created by Dr. William Moulton Marston, is that she was sculpted from clay by her mother, Queen Hippolyta, and gifted with superhuman powers from the Greek gods while being raised as an Amazon. Her alias is Diana Prince, a wartime nurse and military secretary in World War II.[2] The secret identity is known to be the character's alter ego—called the "superhero persona"—and is unveiled when the character is called to protect themselves from pressure or public scrutiny or even to insulate loved ones from their lifestyle and actions.[3]

As we've discussed, Gen-Zers have grown up as digital natives with a keen understanding of various technologies. This early and ongoing exposure to the digital world has meant that Gen-Zers have never known a world without the benefits of such technological tools. So, how can these digital experiences benefit the workplace? In general, Gen-Zers are more likely to extend their workday outside of the office, finishing tasks while commuting, watching or streaming shows, or even while at the gym after work. This also means that Gen-Zers tend to start their day earlier. Most Gen-Zers check their phones for texts, social media notifications, e-mails, and more as soon as they wake up and right before they go to bed. Some also keep their phones on all night and even conduct business while in the restroom. This suggests that one benefit employers receive from Gen-Zers and their double identities is access to them beyond traditional work hours.

The double identity also allows Gen-Zers to embrace the importance of those coworker and client relationships, even when not physically present in the workplace. For those given the option to work outside the office confines, it is often Gen-Zers and millennials who more readily adapt their work to remote environments with little difficulty, while Gen-Xers and baby boomers tend to have a bit more difficulty when making that transition.

Some Gen-Xers, though, are equally up to date with technological advancements because they are often responsible for raising, leading, or mentoring millennials and Gen-Zers. These individuals must also make important decisions about the appropriateness and effectiveness of remote working arrangements for members of their organizations. For example, higher-education institutions continue to shift the balance of traditional in-person learning and working on campus and increased options for online learning and working from home. As a result, faculty who previously had little experience teaching or working in an online environment have required additional guidance in order to adapt. Younger faculty at these same institutions, however, with recent experience with online teaching and working environments, have been ahead of the curve; Gen-Xers and baby boomers both have struggled to identify with and readily adjust to these changes rapidly.

Gen-Zers are quite accustomed to "multitasking" everyday; they consume massive amounts of information across multiple Internet sites and social media platforms simultaneously.[4] Many older generations are doubtful about the effectiveness of this multitasking but often admire millennials and Gen-Zers for their ability to do so and may even rely on them when certain workplace situations arise. Sometimes we must consider the quality of the time spent on devices rather than the quantity of time spent on devices.[5]

With these characteristics in mind, Gen-Zers also face many challenges when dealing with their prominent double identities. Due to 24/7 connectivity, Gen-Zers face increased stress levels and anxiety in these same workplace environments. If stress and anxiety are continually high, then members of this generation may require increased mental health benefits. With the increased awareness of mental health throughout all communities and organizations, employers may have to offer inflated benefits packages to retain Gen-Zers, as well as millennials, and to maintain or increase organizational productivity.

Negative perceptions of other generations are difficult to overcome. One misperception of Gen-Z is that they are too focused on social media and simply cannot focus on specific tasks for an extended period of time. It is important that all colleagues within an organization work to eliminate negative generational perceptions, as they can influence how coworkers treat one another and the broader cross-generational work expectations.[6] For example, Gen-Zers, like millennials before them, often believe that baby boomers and Gen-Xers are not tech-savvy and are not open to evolving the way they approach their jobs. Whether true or not, this statement may make Gen-Zers believe they are more competent than their older coworkers, which can lead to unnecessary friction among colleagues with certain topics (e.g., technology). These beliefs about coworkers of other generations perpetuates to others the idea that one generational cohort is superior to the others—exactly the opposite of the ideal outcome.

Gen-Zers, as well as members of other generations, forget that their online lives and workplace lives require different types of communication, especially when using social media. Gen-Zers use Twitter, Instagram, TikTok, and other social media platforms to express themselves and their opinions, but doing so could potentially violate organizational social media policies by unwittingly affiliating with certain groups, movements, or ideas that run counter to the organization for which they work. Also, a selfie with friends, margaritas in hand, during a work lunch break might prove to be problematic on return to the workplace. Clearly, double identities can benefit the workplace but also must be monitored so they don't negatively affect business productivity.

Just Causes

Gen-Z and millennials have shown a passion, if not a self-imposed obligation, to fight perceived injustices and right the wrongs within their society. We know that "donning their capes" is a motivating factor of employment for members of these generations. With that, it might be beneficial for employers to identify opportunities to support local community events and organizations. Not only do these community interactions strengthen external relationships, but they can also foster internal collegial relationships because coworkers can experience them together. Supporting causes by forming company teams to raise money for an annual 5K walk, volunteering to help with Habitat for Humanity, or implementing a community-based day out are great ways to build relationships within the organization and across the community.

Another important consideration for managers is to promote intergenerational cooperation in order to expand social networks and set a positive tone for effective outcomes. This helps to create a supportive work environment with mutual respect and potentially increased productivity.[7] Also, when job satisfaction is higher, Gen-Zers are more likely to stay with an organization longer; they are not interested in jumping from job to job as quickly as millennials did—they desire job stability and professional growth.[8]

One challenge that Gen-Zers face in their fight for "just causes" is having a variety of community involvement options to support because many social issues change over time. If organizations can seek employee feedback on which community events to attend or causes to support, then Gen-Zers would be able to contribute many ideas and may even take the lead. However, we also know that many Gen-Zers like the stability of having *one* cause that they can focus on in the workplace because it provides much-needed structure in their lives. Feedback about employees' preferences can be beneficial to a multigenerational workplace, especially when Gen-Zers may also hold more than one job.

Second Jobs

Oftentimes, Gen-Zers voluntarily choose to have a second job, even if that position does not reward them monetarily for their efforts. Volunteering within the community can sometimes be seen as a second job, depending on the level of commitment, but this involvement can also help organizations receive further recognition. Because Gen-Zers seek professional growth, their second jobs might easily be based in professional development. For example, we know that Gen-Zers want to learn new skills and improve their knowledge base, even outside of their organizational commitments. Many Gen-Zers take free or low-cost courses or earn certificates on the Internet, learning at their own pace and applying their newly refined skills or know-how.

A clear challenge resulting from holding a second job is that many Gen-Zers have accrued student loan debt and are often just starting to support themselves. This means that they may have another part-time job, side hustle, gig, or even another full-time job just to pay the bills. This is taxing. Their sleep deprivation could eventually affect their daily workplace productivity. Couple that with the stress and anxiety that many feel, and Gen-Zers may burn out quickly and require mental health days or increased personal time off (PTO). Their superpower or ability to seek out and hold a second job may actually be an Achilles' heel.

Extraordinary Powers or Abilities

As previously mentioned, tech-savviness is Gen-Z's prominent superpower. They are not afraid to try new platforms, mobile or desktop devices, and social media outlets as they are unveiled. Members of this generation are willing to take the time to play with these new forms of technology, apps, and programs in order to understand their limitations and abilities. They are comfortable enough not to worry about losing data or even sharing data if the technology can ease some burden in their lives. Gen-Zers often spend their free time learning new ways to use these technological advancements. They adapt rapidly when their favorite new app, smartphone, program, or video game becomes passé.[9]

One downside to this extraordinary power is that the desire for immediacy has increased among Gen-Zers. Attention spans are decreasing, and memory is being replaced with artificial intelligence (AI), such as Siri, Google, Alexa, and more. *Google* has become the new synonym for *research*, but when Gen-Zers Google important information, they often don't understand the commercialization of search engine optimization (SEO) practices, such as Internet and Google ads and keyword prioritization, are often neglected or ignored. In other words, their lack of fear in using technology is often accompanied by an absence of media literacy. It is when facing these types of adversities that Gen-Zers show their vulnerabilities, including their heightened fallibility.

Adversity

As the worldwide COVID-19 pandemic affected the lives of billions of people throughout 2020, both corporate and education-based organizations, including small and not-for-profit businesses, were forced to accommodate prolonged distance arrangements while adhering to government-mandated quarantines. Those learners and workers already accustomed to an online environment very easily made the adjustment to learning and working from home. However, a large majority of entire populations struggled mightily to maintain comportment online. Not surprisingly, Gen-Zers and other generational cohorts who had no reason to prepare for this shift were easily frustrated by technological woes, including bandwidth restrictions, servers overwhelmed with online traffic, and access to accurate information. Many were fearful and inadequately prepared to shift to such a *mandated* online world while sequestered in their homes, and many defied the mandate. While Gen-Zers may have been able to adapt to such an online workplace environment and may have even enjoyed working from home, they still missed the in-person contact that such a crisis imparted, leading to increased stress and anxiety for them and their loved ones.

Immediately related to the global pandemic, Gen-Zers also had to deal with the economic impact: Those individuals who were recently hired were often the first ones to be furloughed or let go from their newly obtained positions. The economic adversity this generation had already faced with their accumulating debt was exacerbated by a country experiencing a rapidly rising unemployment rate and severely limited health-care benefits. One thing for sure is that Gen-Zers are facing these adversities at an incredibly young age and are witnessing an attempt to adapt entire workforces to virtual environments. Younger Gen-Zers and the generation that follows should now be more prepared to handle future world crises and their impacts on education and the workplace.

Fallibility

As we are aware, all humans are fallible, despite what each generation may believe about its younger self. Employers must remember that, too, about their Gen-Z employees—they will make mistakes. The key to making and benefitting from mistakes is to ensure that employers and coworkers focus on turning negatives into positives so that everyone can learn from their mistakes. If employers have built the concept of risk assessment into their organizational culture, then they can often anticipate how and where employees might show their fallibility.

While Gen-Zers are always seeking more important tasks to complete, it is *not* often in an organization's best interest to put a single person in charge of a task that can potentially take down the organization as a whole—that's just bad business acumen. However, Gen-Zers also need to learn how to fail and then recover, so some built-in risk is expected, even necessary. Mentoring Gen-Zers and others during these moments of fallibility allows them to problem solve and seek assistance from others. Gen-Zers are eager to learn and to please, so organizations must use their enthusiasm to help them through their unwanted and often unrecognized fallibility.

One way to address learning from mistakes is to ensure that mentoring programs are included as part of the organizational culture. Another approach is to have a clearly written policy or organizational handbook outlining risks that are encouraged and discouraged and introducing these risk discussions in the onboarding process. While it is nice to have employees express their independence and creativity, it is important to clearly define consequences so those who embrace their independence and even go rogue can be reined in and get back on track.

Independence

Gen-Zers have showcased independence from early ages, especially as social media platforms grow and creativity is encouraged, and the need for such a skill is becoming an expectation, even in the workplace. This independence is often bolstered by an undying confidence in their own abilities. Gen-Zers are DIY-ers (do-it-yourself-ers) who have discovered and used a wealth of knowledge found in free courses, certifications, and how-to videos.[10] In the workplace, Gen-Zers believe they are ready and able to tackle any assignment or project and confident that they will complete it successfully.

Their independence has also been bolstered by their belief in the value of expressing their individuality to others who may be more settled in their ways. Creativity has moved on the World Economic Forum's list from number 10 in 2015 to number 3 in 2020.[11] However, we also know that Gen-Zers are often not prepared for solving challenging problems, may not be strong interpersonal communicators, and may lack the essential critical thinking for effectively completing an assignment or project. Their independence often leads to a lot of creative ideas, but the output can make them more dependent on their coworkers and employers. Gen-Zers want regular, if not daily, face-to-face interactions with their coworkers and employers, and they rely on feedback to keep them motivated and on track. So while they can work alone, ironically, their independence is really a team effort. Their perceived independence and reliance on others' feedback is a paradox that influences leadership in the workplace.

GENERATION Z IN THE WORKPLACE: SHOULD SUPERHEROES LEAD AND BE LED?

As with most superheroes, who pride themselves on independence, many Gen-Zers enjoy and embrace independence. Unlike millennials, who like to work "on" teams (only when their individual work is recognized by superiors and coworkers) but not "in" groups, Gen-Zers prefer to be "next to" their peers or coworkers and do what is commonly called side-by-side social learning—where everyone may be working individually on their own projects but are also physically present in the same space.

Those born prior to millennials lived and thrived in an interpersonal world, where group work was often expected and technology was limited to pen and paper or maybe a desktop computer. These generations are more adept at interpersonal communication than their younger millennial and Gen-Z counterparts, so they embrace group and teamwork. However, millennials and Gen-Zers have lived in a digital world that has changed the concept of group work as we know it, and side-by-side learning and working appears to be the preference of Gen-Zers. So, how does this preference influence leadership in the workplace?

We identify leadership preferences among millennials in *The Millennial Mindset* and extrapolate these preferences when considering Gen-Z.[12] The following is a definition of *leadership*, followed by a brief discussion of two leadership styles that we believe should be embraced in the twenty-first century to assist employers and coworkers when leading and being led by Gen-Z.

Leadership

Leadership is defined as a "process whereby an individual can influence a group of individuals to achieve a common goal."[13] Notice how this definition does not include someone's age, position, sex, or time on the job. Instead, this definition acknowledges that the key to leadership is *influence*. That *influence* can be had via one's power currencies that are valued by others *at that time*, but it can change from project to project and must not always be assumed by those with certain titles, such as CEOs or supervisors. Instead, influence is contextually based such that influence (thereby leadership) changes over time, place, and project.

Daniel Goleman, an emotional intelligence thought leader, would suggest that one characteristic that is common across those we would label "leaders" is emotional intelligence: a combination of "self-awareness, self-regulation, motivation, empathy and social skill."[14] Awareness of self, other, and situation fit best with the following discussion of two leadership styles.

While there are many styles addressed in leadership literature, we focus on a combination of two styles for millennials—alternating leadership and service leadership—which we believe, with one caveat: Increased feedback, often immediate, is expected whether one is leading or being led. Alternating leadership is characterized by the notion that relying on one leader for all projects is not acceptable or advantageous. Instead, leaders should take the reins when their skill sets and expertise demand a leadership role, so everyone can potentially be a leader on a project or task; the expertise or influence must be valued *at that time*. Service leadership is bound by the aforementioned rule of thumb, whereby the greater good of the organization is primary, and different people are needed to serve the organization or its constituencies at various times and for various tasks. The idea of "service to others" strikes a positive chord with both millennials and Gen-Zers. They don't want annual work assessments; instead, they want ongoing feedback, not control, from leaders, like coaches, who can be honest and transparent in their guidance, so they grow and be of service to the organization.[15]

What we learn from Gen-Z's superhero characteristics is that although they are independent, they are fallible; although they are independent, they can work in teams; and because they are independent, they may be good leaders *at times*. They need others' feedback and guidance to work toward achieving professional goals. They want to face criticism head on, not be pampered (face adversity), as long as the criticism is done privately.[16]

These characteristics suggest that Gen-Z can lead, be team players, or be led. Sometimes they need to be led by others with more experience, different powers or abilities, and time on the job in order to achieve professional growth. But sometimes, those things may not be as important as the skills or knowledge a person, including a Gen-Zer, may bring to the project *at that time*. In our view, leadership should no longer be considered static and ongoing; instead, leadership must be dynamic, so that effective changes are made according to the context and betterment of the workplace. Just as products and services need to be tailored to them, so must leadership. This *customizable leadership*, our new type of leadership, may be the best way to proceed.

Generation-Z is primed to lead and be led under the right circumstances via a customizable leadership style. We can suggest that employers tout the importance of generational competence in the workplace so that they do not leave one or more generation behind. More importantly, Gen-Z superheroes can "don their capes" as needed to the benefit of the organization as a whole.

FIGHTING FOR
A CAUSE

Understanding Gen-Z's Purpose

*"It takes real character to admit one's failures—and not a
little of wisdom to remember, this man's world of yours will
never be without pain and suffering until it learns love,
and respect for human rights. Keep your hands extended to
all in friendliness but never holding the gun of persecution
and intolerance!"—Wonder Woman*

As with late baby boomers and early Gen-Xers, Generation Z is understandably similar in their views about social, environmental, and
political causes. Members of this generational cohort are quick to take to
the streets for a good cause, whether it be walking out of school to protest a
nearby landfill; marching for lesbian, gay, bisexual, trans, queer, questioning, intersex, asexual, and pansexual (LGBTQ+) rights; or protesting police
brutality. Gen-Z is not only willing to be seen, but they also encourage others
and take leadership roles in many instances.

We should remember that Gen-Z is often influenced by its sometimes-
liberal-slanted views of free speech. Authors Greg Lukianoff and Jonathan
Haidt remind us that many millennials and Gen-Zers have limited views
of free speech, which often means *their* free speech about acceptance and

tolerance, not necessarily the free speech of those who oppose such ideas (i.e., White nationalists and Black Israelites in recent news).[1] Despite their apparent flaw in judgment, parents and guardians, employers, and educators need to be aware of the causes this generation stands up for and supports and then find ways to leverage these interests in the classroom and the workplace.

While millennials tend to be more tolerant of various socialistic-leaning ideologies, (e.g., supporting Bernie Sanders), Gen-Z seems to take a step back, albeit a small one, and focus more on the political systems' positions rather than on simple party lines. It was no wonder that Bernie Sanders was a stalwart in his run for Democratic presidential candidate in 2016 and saw his numbers rise in his run for the same position in 2020. In 2019 and 2020, we witnessed a variety of diverse candidates throw their hats into the political ring during the primaries, including Kamala Harris, Pete Buttigieg, Corey Booker, and Andrew Yang.[2] While many were unable to raise enough funds to be on the debate stage and continue their pursuits, their presence grabbed the attention of Gen-Z. As a result, Gen-Z has the potential to play a major role in the current state of US politics by casting their votes, as so many millennials failed to cast theirs in 2016. The time is now for Gen-Z to embrace their country's future and get out the vote.

This chapter highlights issues and challenges that Gen-Zers face during these tumultuous times. In a sense, these causes are their nemeses or villains that they have shown are worthy of their time to fight against.

JUST CAUSES

A just cause is one that individuals view as morally and ethically right. For example, ownership and control of one's own body is a just cause because it recognizes the importance and inalienable right to make personal decisions, especially when they do not harm others. There are three categories of just causes for Gen-Zers today: social, environmental, and political. While others may include additional areas of just causes, we believe that these three categories are identifiable in today's cultural discourse. Not all of Gen-Z's pertinent causes are discussed, but here are a few to get you started.

Social Activism

In the Trump era, the loss of diversity, acceptance, and tolerance in the United States is on the rise. With what many acknowledge as a weak role model for diverse views and lives, Trump has raised both ire and support during his tumultuous first term as president. The apparent political divide is one of clear partisanship: Congressional members vote along party lines, with few exceptions (e.g., Republican senator Mitt Romney during the February 2020 impeachment trial).

In a country built on immigration, the abundance of diverse people across racial, ethnic, religious, sexual, and socioeconomic lines is still absolute, although this diversity is more readily scrutinized by xenophobes, who fear that which they do not know. Historically, the United States has been perceived as a country founded on freedom, which is cyclically challenged by the broader population (racial and gender adversities, religious and White supremacists, gun rights and control activism). Clearly, the United States is struggling to maintain its reputation as the land of the free and must now fight an increasingly negative perception, including one that harkens back to the hate of the 1930s and early 1940s.

Many states have legalized same-sex marriage and implemented bail-reform programs to help the economically challenged; however, diversity is still a primary focus for many people but dismissed by so many others, so much so that acceptance and tolerance are often considered taboo. But many Gen-Zers are out in front of these social issues and have put on their capes and used their powers to realign the course of history for the preservation of their collective futures. Bam! Pow! Gen-Zers must fight for and engage many social issues, especially social justice, to change the world and secure their futures. It is a global uphill battle.

Social Justice

Here we are in 2020, almost sixty years post–civil rights, and yet racial tensions are still high. Many people may have assumed that passing legislation in the 1950s and 1960s would have ended injustice and inequality, but that is not accurate. Gen-Zers are growing up during a time when terrorism, both domestically and abroad, is an everyday occurrence. They have grown up

CHAPTER 5

with negative media messaging about Muslims, debates about LGBTQ+ rights, and unequal pay for women; they know that equality does not mean that all people are treated equally.

Members of this generation experience further inequalities in ways that may not immediately come to mind. They have experienced and identified racial profiling, anti-Semitism, and hate crimes, which is again on the rise, and they recognize that classism is on the public agenda (e.g., tax cuts for the wealthy). #MeToo, #BlackLivesMatter, #TransRightsMatter, and more are continuously trending in the digiverse. Gen-Z has even witnessed a US president mocking people with disabilities and exhibiting sexist and racist behaviors, with other world leaders exhibiting similar behavior (e.g., Canadian prime minister Justin Trudeau).[3] #StopTheHate has been on the minds of many, but social conservatism appears to be strengthening. The annual Accelerating Acceptance report "shocked the country with a statistic that young Americans are growing less supportive of the LGBTQ+ movement, while College Pulse reported that only a quarter of Gen Z students support abortion under any circumstance."[4]

Gen-Zers need only look to *Guardians of the Galaxy* to see diversity: "Each member of the multi-racial, multi-species team has its role. There's the half-human, half-alien Peter Quill/Star-Lord; the green-skinned female alien Gamora; the superhuman, blue-skinned and red-tattooed Drax the Destroyer; Groot, an extraterrestrial tree monster; and the genetically engineered half-raccoon, half-man Rocket. They all work together."[5] Superheroes transcend issues to work together for the greater good. Comic book narratives offer Gen-Zers insights into social justice topics. Now more than ever, the youngest generation needs to lead change and engage in public discourse; Gen-Z, the foot soldiers of our times, must don their superhero capes and do so in the public eye.

Examples of those who have already stepped up to challenge include

- Malala Yousafzai, who received a Nobel Peace Prize at age seventeen and has been fighting for women's educational rights for years[6];
- Jazz Jennings, a transgender teen who has been fighting for trans rights for more than a decade[7];
- Jaden Smith, son of actors Will Smith and Jada Pinkett, pridefully using his celebrity platform to foreground gender fluidity and LGBTQ+ rights[8];

- Argentinian teens, who in 2019 fought for gender inclusivity in the Spanish language[9];
- Kaitlin Bennett, who is fighting for gun rights in opposition to gun control[10]; and
- Tony Weaver, founder and CEO of Weird Enough Productions, who focuses on "offering positive representations of black men, aiming to combat all the issues that negative public perception can lead to: economic disadvantage, police aggression, longer jail sentences, and a distorted sense of black achievement."[11]

The future is bright for Gen-Zers taking a stand for their causes, liberal or conservative; donning their capes; and pulling back the veil of social injustice.

Gun Control

While there are many individuals who responsibly use guns, Gen-Z has grown up witnessing worldwide terrorist acts and mass shootings, both in the United States and abroad. While Gen-Xers may have practiced air raid drills in elementary school, Gen-Zers have lived in a world where their personal safety has been threatened by frequent mass shootings in their schools, where they are supposed to be safest. Additionally, other mass shootings and acts of domestic terrorism have been conducted by human villains, generally using assault rifles, AR-15s, with bump stocks (now banned).[12] This ban will not end mass shootings, but gun control and regulation reform are of great interest for the majority of Gen-Zers.

At Marjorie Stoneman Douglas High School, days after a mass shooting took place, survivors took to the road to get out their message, started a movement, and created the hashtag #NeverAgain. These Gen-Z survivors brought immediate attention to the gun control debate in the United States, and the debate is ongoing. Those who promote gun rights are often attacked or silenced by gun control activists, and vice versa.[13] Only one year after the shooting of February 14, 2019, the *Washington Post* reported that interest and commitment to the #NeverAgain movement had decreased to preshooting levels. Public debate is still needed, and Gen-Zers need to work on their debate and life skills for legislative changes to take hold.

Poverty and Minimum Wage

In the last two decades, people have raised concerns about the economy and the impact the recession has had on many Gen-Zers. During this time, countless people lost jobs, homes, and livelihoods as the economy spiraled downward. Poverty, an ongoing crisis in the United States, became a reality for those unaccustomed to it. Jobs were scarce; unemployment, high; and the outlook, bleak—perhaps not as bleak as the Great Depression but close.

Additionally, the cost of living continues to rise by about 3 percent each year, but Social Security benefits lag behind that growth, and many employers haven't provided their employees raises in years. As a result, baby boomer and early Gen-Xer retirees are reentering the workforce so they can simply survive. Health-care costs have skyrocketed, healthy food costs have increased due to climate change and trade wars, and pay is stagnant for most. Pensions have gone bankrupt, and Social Security has been on and off the cutting board for the past decade. With the average life span of Americans increasing (women live, on average, four to five years longer than men), retiring at 62 is no longer a real option for many people.[14]

For young people in many cities looking to start a job, not a career, in the service or food industry, the minimum wage has increased to fifteen dollars per hour. These types of jobs are now becoming careers for people of all ages, especially those working to stay above the poverty line. As of January 2020, the poverty rate declined, but there was "1.4 million fewer poor people than in 2017. . . . [O]ne in eight Americans still lived below the poverty line—$25,465 for a family with two adults and two children."[15]

Millennials are taking second, even third, jobs to pay off student loan debt, buy homes, and support their families. Taco Bell announced in January 2020 a plan to offer six-figure management jobs ($100,000), a move that is highly unusual in the fast-food industry, where people often can get jobs.[16] The goal of such an initiative is to keep employees longer and prepare them for upper-level management opportunities.

However, there are those Gen-Zers who have been instrumental in bringing attention to particular causes, including kindergartner Katelynn Hardee, who raised money selling "cider, cocoa, and cookies," and other anonymous donors who wiped out student meal debt across the country.[17] When the top twenty-six money makers own more than the bottom 50 percent of all people in the world, concerns arise for those less fortunate.[18]

Cost of Higher Education and Health Care

Higher education is at a crossroads as well. Immense student loan debt, with the hope that the sacrifice will unlock better-paying jobs, is the norm. Costs to attend college rose by 37 percent between 2008 and 2018, and for many eighteen- to twenty-four-year-olds, college is quickly becoming cost prohibitive.[19] It is hard to be an agent of change (superhero) if you can't pay the bills or afford a higher education.

As millennials completed their high school degrees and enrolled in colleges in huge numbers, higher-education institutions evolved and tried to meet consumer needs. All the while, tuition and housing costs continued to increase as federal and state funding dramatically decreased or even was shut down. While millennials on average carry the third-largest student loan debt than any other generation, their fear of lifelong indebtedness overrides their optimism.

The recession in the late 2000s didn't help their cause because their late-baby-boomer and early-Gen-X parents were no longer able to pay for their children's college education. Additionally, many late Gen-Xers and early millennials focused more on their careers and delayed starting families, so much so that higher education is anticipated to experience decreased enrollments for college-aged children. Colleges and universities reacted to this prediction by focusing on education customization, where students are provided more flexibility with their educational journeys. The multimedia, hyperconnected world that Gen-Zers live in demands different knowledge than traditional liberal arts, which are focused purely on language, history, and literature. Instead, entrepreneurial programs, e-sports communication and competition, and social media courses across disciplines are now mainstream. This educational shift began with later millennials and has persisted with Gen-Zers, who are not always willing to shell out big bucks for a degree with little return.

Students are now in the driver's seat because they want a tangible return on their educational investment (ROI). The big *C*, *customization*, discussed in chapter 3, became quite prominent in the last decade. Colleges and universities across the country have cut liberal arts programs while focusing on science, technology, education, and math (STEM) courses that could be put into practice upon graduation, often leading to higher starting salaries.

Similarly, the ROI that Gen-Zers demand for their health care is also extremely important. Increases in costs of prescription drugs, health plans, Medicare, and even long-term health care are in this generation's crosshairs. In today's workplace, fewer employers are able to cover the full cost of health care, and retirement health-care coverage is often a fantasy. Millennials initiated the urgent call for health-care overhaul in 2016 when they supported Bernie Sanders. Then, baby boomers jumped onboard as they realized their anticipated pensions would fail to cover living and health-care costs until Social Security benefits could be applied. Elder care and medical care have improved, but the life spans of adults are considerably longer than when Social Security was first implemented, placing increasing pressure on the federal government to lower health-care costs for all.

The current divide among the haves and have-nots is becoming increasingly obvious, as many who make and have more money don't always want to foot the bill for the more economically challenged people. As a result, political tension surrounding health care has played out in the 2020 election, and Gen-Z will face an uphill battle in having affordable health care for themselves and their families. Many will choose to ultimately forgo health insurance, especially when medical information can increasingly be found in the digiverse.

Environmental Warriors

When climate change comes up in conversation, debate typically ensues. Many believe that climate change is a nonfactor in earth's longevity, yet most Gen-Zers are closely aligned with millennials in their commitment to saving the world. From sustainable energy to plastics in landfills and the ocean to animal rights and more, Gen-Zers are leading the charge and encouraging their parents and guardians to start doing their part, as well.

The attention to climate activism continues to rise as widespread environmental challenges are realized on a daily basis. California has been hampered by widespread fires and drought; the 2020 Australia brush fires killed billions of wildlife and severely damaged the broader ecostructure; volcanic eruptions have occurred in both the Philippines and Hawaii; powerful freak storms have wreaked havoc in Europe, across the United States, and globally; increasing temperatures are melting glaciers in Antarctica and Alaska at an unprecedented rate; and the earth experienced its second-warmest year to date in 2019.[20]

Gen-Z doesn't need to make a hard rhetorical case for climate change because they are witnessing it each and day around the globe. Greta Thunberg, a Gen-Z leader and activist, has been fighting climate change worldwide and was even voted *Time* magazine's 2019 person of the year. Her influence demonstrates to us all just how effective social media and in-person presence can be in calling for and leading change, even at a young age; her cape has been on for a few years now, and the cause needs her to keep fighting the climate change villains.

Concerns over oil pipelines crossing state borders within the United States and about oil production, both in the United States and abroad (e.g., Iran and Saudi Arabia), raise issues about sustainable energy and the larger consequences of oil-related disasters on water and farming sources.[21] For example, fallout from the Deepwater Horizon's gulf coast oil-drilling explosion in 2010 has recently escalated, years after the explosion, because the amount of damage to the gulf was severely underestimated or covered up.[22] Environmental events and disasters such as these are real and pertinent, and Gen-Z has the most to lose if change doesn't happen at all levels, including politics.

Political Advocates

The United States is at a unique crossroads in its political history, as partisanship has become the norm. Beyond partisanship, freedom in the United States is now also under deeper scrutiny. The role of the press as the "Fourth Estate," or watchdog, has been questioned, and the national scene is also being reflected in the collegiate press over the past forty years: "State and federal courts have decided over 60 cases in the last four decades directly involving censorship of the public college and university student press. The decisions have been unanimous in their agreement that the First Amendment forbids almost all censorship of student-edited publications by school administrators."[23] The Trump administration has repeatedly called such newspapers as the *New York Times* and the *Washington Post* "fake news" sources and biased journalism outlets, thus raising questions about the viability of a free and watchful press in the United States moving forward.

Additionally, the right to choose or right to life debate usually holds along party lines, but pro-life voices are growing, perhaps contrary to media reports, as many Gen-Zers are marching for the rights of the unborn and not the right to choose.[24] A 2018 Gallup poll indicates that the number of self-identified pro-life and pro-choice supporters are now about equal (48 percent each), but media coverage suggests that pro-choice supporters make up a larger group than their pro-life counterparts because they are perceived as more accepting and tolerant of people's rights.[25] The stories being told and created in our media demand more discussion, yet not many Gen-Zers are prepared for debate through civil discourse.

Partisanship has also influenced the voting process. The 2020 Iowa primary was, by all definitions, chaotic to say the least, as the final results took weeks to sort out, with no clear winner. Judgments are now made before the outcomes of elections, at both the local and national levels: that elections are rigged and even that foreign influence on the democratic process has merit, calling our democracy into question.

Partisan gerrymandering, where districts are redrawn in favor of one group over another, are quite common in the United States but not illegal.[26] Couple that with some voters being turned away from the polls and voter reforms, and the current political system may be on the brink of demise.[27] The 2016 US presidential election was tumultuous, while the 2020 election may ultimately generate further cracks in the foundation of government.

The potential for change is upon us, as millennials and Gen-Zers will likely hold the largest voting voice in 2020, and their decisions will determine the future of America; let's hope they don their capes and vote in 2020. This heavy burden lies on the shoulders of so many young people, and their participation is a necessity, not an option. Parents, guardians, employers, and educational institutions are in unique positions to assist and positively influence Gen-Z in keeping democracy and civil discourse alive, well, and living in America.

SUGGESTIONS FOR INTERACTING WITH GEN-Z

Parenting

Many of today's parents are just as addicted to their phones as their millennial or Gen-Z children. Surprisingly, Gen-Zers even question the amount of time that their parents or guardians are spending staring at their tablets, laptops, smartwatches, and smartphones. The amount of time parents and guardians are spending on these devices is, in fact, shaping the relationships they have with their children and others. Quality time is now often spent texting, face-timing, and engaging others digitally, either face to face (FtF) via visual technologies or digitally via chats, texts, and social media platforms.

One way that parents and guardians can engage their children is by having conversations about social, environmental, and political issues that they are exposed to. Additionally, it is still important for parents to engage with their children by going to events, museums, and marches and spending more *in-person and together time*. Doing so will improve their Gen-Zers' current and future interactions in the real world, face to face—not just digitally. In other words, be physically present, untethered for a time, to get to know your Gen-Zers—without technology. You not only will connect on a personal level, but you also will improve your Gen-Zers' life skills, thus aiding them in becoming more capable and competent participants in their everyday lives, acting as the much need foot soldiers of change.

Workplace

Employers must recognize how important social, environmental, and political causes are to members of this generation. Gen-Z employees often seek organizations that give back to or raise money for larger causes, such as Habitat for Humanity, Race for a Cause, and Make a Wish, or offer charitable services. Employers who take an interest in people, events, and communities outside of potential profitability for the company appeal widely to Gen-Zers, many of whom have been volunteering or advocating for a large part of their lives. Participation in these charitable organizations on behalf of the company via team relays, walks, and other outlets entice Gen-Zers. They are interested in giving back to the community and believe corporations bear that responsibility. In fact, corporate responsibility and transparency may be more important than the almighty dollar when Gen-Zers make employment decisions.

Classroom

Educators are also in a unique position to build quality relationships with and teach responsibility to their students. From the age of five, most US children spend more time with educators than they do their parents or guardians in an average week. This places educators in a unique position: facilitating the growth of informed and ethical citizens. While many states mandate "teaching to the test" as a result of the No Child Left Behind Act (see chapter 8), educators can incorporate current social, environmental, and political discussions into their teaching. With problem-based education still a focus in precollege learning, discussions about key global issues are relevant to Gen-Zers' intellectual and cultural growth. For example, a fifth-grade lesson about climate can introduce the complexities of climate change. Students then can discuss in class the responsibilities and potential impacts of human involvement and develop a policy that can make a difference locally.

Clearly, the participation of all generations in sustaining democracy and changing the current social path is prudent. Rather than place blame on any single generation, now is the time to work together for change,. We all have work to do, so we need to dust off our capes and fight for survival.

6

KNOW YOUR SUPERHEROES

Teaching and Learning in a Gen-Z Environment

*"The greatest power on Earth is the magnificent power
we, all of us, possess . . . the power of the human brain!"*
—*Professor X*

Like a superhero, each member of a society requires help from their family or peers over the course of each day, and Generation Z is no different. Although they are quite entrepreneurial, many lack both the soft skills necessary for effective communication and the critical-thinking and problem-solving skills needed for achieving educational and professional success. In this chapter we offer an overview of how Gen-Z's superhero characteristics influence pedagogy and learning. Regardless if members of Gen-Z are identified metaphorically as superheroes, the fact remains that they, too, can benefit by refining particular skills. Additionally, despite everything they think they know, members of this generation largely seek out strong role models and mentors but should also be willing to serve a similar role to others, regardless of age. Therefore, we offer a quick overview of previous generations and their educational journeys.

CHAPTER 6

A LOOK BACK

As noted earlier, historical events shape each generation in unique ways, including politically, environmentally, economically, and ideologically. Our focus in this chapter is educationally. Traditionalists and members of the silent generation experienced the end of World Wars I and II and saw their families recover during the Depression (silent generation members). Large numbers of veterans returned from global conflicts, looking to pick up their old jobs where they left off, and benefitted from military educational programs set up by the US government. These individuals looked to establish their homes and settle down in the suburbs as housing became more affordable. Both generations were taught in environments where teachers were valued and respected, while students sat, listened, and learned, often quite passively. Learning core knowledge and facts about the world, the government, and the Western canon was all the rage; diversity, not so much.[1]

Then along came the baby boomers, born to early traditionalists after the war. As the world settled from these conflicts, this generation benefitted from a healthy economic upturn made possible by careers that paid well and allowed most to "keep up with the Joneses." There was also more talk of the American dream, with its clearly defined gender roles presented throughout media outlets. Racial tensions were brewing, and distinctions between men's work and women's work were primary, as few men became nurses or K–12 teachers.

In the early 1950s, women were still limited in their educational and career goals. They were mostly encouraged to become teachers if they worked outside the home so that they could still raise their children, thus embracing the cultural norms of the times. This oppressive societal system for those not privileged by their race, class, gender, or sexual orientation promoted overt discrimination.

Even in wealthy families, despite their education and societal upbringing, women were still expected to settle down, marry, and have children, with their husbands continuing to be the household breadwinner. Popular culture, especially TV, reflected these norms in shows like *Father Knows Best*, *Leave It to Beaver*, *I Love Lucy*, and many others. Women were portrayed in domestic environments, with fewer Rosie the Riveters than during the wars. Instead, hospitals and classrooms became their acceptable workspaces.

Members of the LGBTQ+ communities were also silenced, willingly or unwillingly, and often forced to assimilate. Those who were caught or found guilty by association (a leftover fear from McCarthyism ideology) lost their jobs, homes, and lives; many were imprisoned, sent to psychiatric hospitals, or even "converted" to heterosexuality and forced to conform to numerous social, sexual, and gender norms. These tumultuous times also affected the educational system.

In the 1950s and '60s, increasing racial tensions brought numerous US legal cases to the forefront, including *Brown v. Board of Education* in 1954, where segregation of schools was declared unconstitutional.[2] These court cases opened many educational doors for minority groups, especially African Americans, in the United States and changed the classroom dynamic from that point forward. However, the door opened very slowly and didn't end discrimination, especially in blended schools, where African American children put themselves in harm's way every day to pursue a better education.

Around the same time these racial challenges were escalating, television sets also became more widespread in middle- and upper-class homes, becoming the primary mechanism for consuming mass media. Such events as desegregation were now available for viewing by the larger population, including the sit-in at a Greensboro Woolworth's and the Little Rock Nine, both of which were covered by multiple news stations.[3] Feminism entered its second wave, calling for change and equal rights. The Stonewall Riots paved the way for gay and lesbian rights.[4] It was clear that oppressed groups were now demanding change, garnering coverage, and finding many allies.

Even college campuses became a place for political dissent and activism through the 1960s and 1970s, as college students took the reins for change. However, K–12 educators were still viewed as the authorities who dispensed knowledge to students in the classroom.[5] Children were previously taught to respect the authority of their teachers, to reiterate teachers' knowledge to succeed, and to earn good grades. This expectation continued through the 1980s, with small pockets of educational change emerging throughout.

The late 1960s and early 1970s specifically brought more political unrest to college campuses, with Kent State being most notable.[6] Both in the United States and abroad, political upheavals by college students were becoming more prominent, which deeply affected the educational climate.

Older students, especially those in college, were no longer willing to be passive receptors of knowledge provided by their teachers. They were more willing to dissent and question rather than blindly follow. Teaching also became more challenging yet again, as the makeup of the student body was changing.

Educational changes were slow to take hold, but it wasn't until the late 1980s and early 1990s, that they would become more apparent. Electronic and mobile technologies were becoming more popular and available, and home computers were steadily on the rise.[7] Unbeknownst to many, the Internet was also just a few years away. Gen-Xers were considered culturally illiterate for not knowing classic literature and music, world history, and cultural references. Many were shamed by their elders for how little they knew, especially of the Western canon that had been prioritized for decades.[8] However, let's be honest: each generation is questioned by its predecessors about what it knows and what it is capable of, and so a popular culture divide emerged in the late 1980s.

Enter the 2000s, and cultural literacy, a baby boomer leftover, was replaced (or more aptly, *updated*) by not only immediately available information but also increasingly diverse knowledge. Because the Western canon was most prominent in the US educational system in the nineteenth and twentieth centuries, twenty-first-century parents, educators, and children demanded multicultural texts and lessons to better represent the world and historical events. This continued throughout the 2000s, when anyone with mobile and home technology could find several resources on a topic in a moment's notice. Suddenly, simple recall of the Western canon and other cultural information was not as important as access to that information. The cultural literacy question became, "Why do I need to know or remember this when I can look it up right now?"

This question resonates even today, with more than 95 percent of Gen-Zers owning smartphones and using them during class.[9] Additionally, educators themselves have smartphones, especially millennial and Gen-X teachers. Educators have always adapted to new methods for reaching students over time, from industrialization through the technology prominent today. The ability to adapt is increasingly important in today's classrooms, as well, not only for teachers, but also for students and their parents and guardians.

LEVERAGING SUPERHERO CHARACTERISTICS IN THE CLASSROOM: REACHING AND TEACHING GEN-Z

The rest of this chapter expands on the multiple superhero characteristics previously introduced and uses these as a framework to contextualize potential changes and adaptations over time. Educators may have their own thoughts about who needs to change in the classroom, but knowledge of these superhero characteristics can be leveraged in the classroom to aid both teaching and learning. With students and teachers collaborating in the learning process, understanding the importance of these double identities can lead the way for change.

Double Identity

The first superhero characteristic is double identity. No matter your age or cultural background, educators must realize that they, too, have double, if not more, identities to maintain. Educators in the classroom are generally different when they are the colleague in the teacher's lounge, where they are not always knowledgeable about lunchtime discussion topics. Couple this non-teaching identity with their identities as friends, family, partners, and more, both in person *and* online, and identity is equally complex for educators and their students. In today's fast-paced world, where immediacy is expected, creativity is sometimes forgotten in the classroom. What was once a place to don creative teaching hats became restricted heading into the early 2000s.

The now-defunct 2001 No Child Left Behind Act focused on K–12 education during Gen-Z's primary school years and on "teaching to the test." Opponents of No Child Left Behind felt constrained by evaluations largely based on test results. Their identities as *good* teachers were questioned, with more importance given to student outcomes, despite the many other factors influencing a student's test scores. However, there were opportunities within this initiative for both personal and developmental student growth, especially with a clear focus on disadvantaged groups.[10]

How one teaches content is as important as the *content* one teaches. Nuanced communication and delivering necessary materials has broadened to assist children in developing beyond simple memorization of facts. For example, a third-grade lesson on historical figures may encompass a more diverse list, including texts like *What Would She Do? 25 True Stories of Trailblazing Rebel Women*, to raise awareness and provide a deeper understanding of the role women have played throughout history.[11]

Identity is an important characteristic for teachers and this superhero generation. Now, educators need to use these identities to reach Gen-Z. High school teachers can have their students use Google Voice to text them or hold a review session as a Twitter chat. Additionally, using Gen-Z's passion for just causes is one way to reach them and acknowledge their complex identities.

Just Causes

Prior to the prevalence of the Internet and social media platforms, children were often distanced from societal issues and conflicts *intentionally* so that they could *be* children. Parents and guardians had an easier time restricting television use for their late-baby-boomer and early-Gen-Xer children when there were far fewer televisions in the home. As televisions became more affordable, keeping children away from adult social issues and conflicts portrayed on television became more difficult. Additionally, as kids, many Gen-Xers fended for themselves until an adult arrived home.

Millennials were different. During their lifetime, they experienced television moving from analog to digital and from over air to cable. Television also began to take a back seat to the Internet, where millennials could communicate, play, and advocate with friends without having to leave their homes. Broadcast television stations were, and still are, more highly monitored and regulated than any cable network or streaming service available today. The inability to access information aimed at certain age groups became almost null and void, thus lessening an informational divide that earlier generations had experienced. Today, children can learn, access (even with parental controls), and advocate for a cause or gather information about any topic by simply asking Siri, Google, or Alexa to "tell me about X."

As technology advances, children are exposed to varying issues and ideas with which they may have never encountered in a non-Internet world—which can be simultaneously both detrimental and beneficial. It can be detrimental because children are exposed to things they don't *need* to know about at much younger ages than previous generations were. For example, does a child of ten *need* to be exposed to sexual issues via programming available in the afternoons, such as soap operas and daytime talk shows, or via some video game or website, even YouTube? Children used to go about their lives learning about things at "appropriate ages," and parents and regulators were content in controlling that access and determining that age.

On the flip side, now that children have 24/7 access from an early age, a benefit is increased awareness of social, environmental, and cultural issues. These issues can be put to good use in the classroom, providing opportunities for improving digital literacy, critical thinking, and perspective taking. Trending stories about poor or poisoned water sources in Flint, Michigan, and Hoosick Falls, New York, could be discussed with elementary school students learning about water sources, the planet, and climate change.

Certainly, educators can find ways to include pertinent just causes in their lesson plans. Doing so can also make Gen-Zers aware of social problems, encourage research and discussion, and even provide students with an opportunity to work on solutions from earlier ages, especially because they have their superhero capes at the ready!

Problem Solving

For many Gen-Zers, recognizing that a problem exists is the first step in their educational process. Once students read about or see a video on an issue, they can work toward addressing that issue through project-based learning.[12] Teachers may find problem-based learning essential in reaching this generation because they can better identify a challenge affecting the local, regional, national, or international levels.

This type of instruction can be implemented at any age, but it must be appropriately adapted to students' cognitive developmental stage. It would be good to initially ask them to write or tell what they know, then have them conduct research and use the assigned course materials to explain the problem and identifying solutions. This means communicating clear learning outcomes. For example, in a higher-education media literacy course, a semester-long project might address this question: "How can our libraries assist local patrons in becoming more media literate?" Some outcomes might be to define *media literacy*, identify what local or campus libraries currently offer in terms of media literacy skill building or creation, and then offer a proposal for change based on the demographics of the locale and the course materials used throughout the semester.

This problem-based assignment may guide students to start the process by conducting the appropriate research, perhaps by even interviewing local librarians and visiting library websites and facilities. However, students must also read the current literature (readings from class and outside of class) about media literacy, formulate a clear working definition of *media literacy*, and then operationalize its characteristics or components to support the research findings. This means providing rationales for library programming and not simply using opinion to do so; two life skills they would also be working on during this assignment would be critical thinking and perspective taking. Simply providing the information is no longer enough for students, and problem-based learning provides customization for learning, an important element for Gen-Zers and necessary for developing perspective taking and empathy.

Collaboration

Oftentimes, reading is a learning activity completed alone. However, problem-based learning emphasizes the need for diverse perspectives in order to identify the best way to address a problem. Typically, using this learning style, problem solving is conducted in groups, which may raise social anxiety and performance concerns among Gen-Z group members. However, this is an opportunity to explain aspects of group work and its viability in solving problems. Most of the time, students are afraid that their group grade may be lowered if one person doesn't complete assigned parts of the project or may not be able to work at a distinctively high level. Educators may choose to have them collaborate but also grade them on individual merit, using a clear grading rubric.

Furthermore, both team building and participation are essential workplace skills, so collaboration has become an essential life skill. Discussions about leadership dynamics, intra- and interpersonal communication, conflict management, and emotional intelligence (EQ) can lead to far broader outcomes then simply noting that they have completed the task. In other words, how they worked through the problem is as important as *that* they offered solutions. Superheroes learn from their experiences to be more efficient and effective in future interactions, and Gen-Z would benefit from this type of metalearning, as well.

Second Job

In the classroom, it is quite easy for students to focus on being students; this is their *one* true job: complete assignments, take quizzes and exams, and earn grades. What is becoming evident with Gen-Zers is that a discussion of what it means to be a student today is necessary, and this involves more than that one true job. Most people can generally excel if they have interest in a topic. One thing that most students don't think about is *their* role in classroom learning, which is actually their *second job* as students. By this we mean that one student job is to complete all graded assignments to the best of their ability, with a secondary job of ensuring that the cultural climate is conducive to learning.

Students want to be challenged and engaged but don't want to do the work it may require to build a positive learning environment. Often, they make statements like "That class is boring" or "That teacher needs to stop talking," without realizing that they are looking externally to the class or teachers to entertain them rather than reflecting on how they are contributing to that environment and their own learning. Teachers do have the responsibility of creating a climate of learning that allows for debate, discussion, and difference, but students also need to actively participate in this environment, whether in person, online, or blended, and should find a passion for the material from intrinsic motivation, not extrinsic.[13]

Students have this second job: to come prepared for discussions of assigned readings at levels that open dialogue among their peers. Teachers must implement methods that help feed their desire to learn—*on their own*. So, while they must perform well as individuals on assignments to earn good grades (extrinsic), they must also enable others, including themselves and their instructors, to be critically and discursively engaged in the classroom (intrinsic). For many educators, teaching has historically meant recall and memorization, and while shifting from this "banking concept" of teaching and learning can be difficult, promoting a continued discussion and debate about the readings can also lead to deeper learning for both teachers and students. A Gen-Z student's second job is just as important as their one true job, and leveraging both contributes to being effective superheroes working toward the greater good (i.e., learning for all). Gen-Zers and teachers need to assist others in unique or extraordinary ways and move away from an "I" to a "We" learning process.

Extraordinary Power or Ability

The superhero-like power or ability that Gen-Zers bring to an educational setting is their connectedness to the digiverse, coupled with their passion for just causes and ability to multitask. They view their ability to use technology as an advantage over their generationally diverse teachers and wholeheartedly believe that they are multitaskers. Educators may disagree with that perception, but they can support these Gen-Zers' self-perceived superhero powers or abilities to assist them in being more technologically literate, thereby enhancing that superpower.

Gen-Zers are quite adept at locating answers quickly. However, many wrongly believe that speed of response is the more important element of their power or ability. Should educators universally adopt smartphones, tablets, or laptops within their classrooms, they must also balance the importance of educating students on how to locate the information from credible sources. Educators must realize that access to these devices may mean these students multitask, simultaneously working on their online identities while completing an assignment, all in the name of FOMO. Additionally, although Gen-Z students may strive to be the first to find information and display this prowess in the classroom, allowing personal technology use in the classroom may lead students away from the prescribed or assigned task and lessen their ability to comprehend and use the information in appropriate and effective ways.

From an educator's perspective, monitoring the technology use of Gen-Zers can be done by roaming the classroom or using applicable software at a teacher's station. Coupling this monitoring with specified tasks, such as finding credible sources or identifying false news, will benefit students in any field or discipline. After all, it is this generation's own credibility that becomes more important as they work their way through school and then into the workplace. To find these quality resources, students must *focus* on the assignment, not on other tangential matters, and educators have a lot to control.

Furthermore, if problem-based or some other proactive learning approach is considered for use in the classroom, then tapping into Gen-Zers' interests in social justice and environmental issues might also encourage them to have more skin in the game. In other words, students would have a *vested* interest. In some cases, the students' understanding of certain issues already exceeds that of the teacher, providing an opportunity for teachers to learn from students; the idea of the sage on the stage in education is shelved, at least some of the time.

Another approach to teaching and learning exists and has now made its way into the dialogue: universal design for learning (UDL). Universal design takes into consideration both the online world as well as the physical world. It has been used in many elementary, middle, and high schools before making its way onto universities and colleges and is focused on the "why, what, and how people learn."[14] What began as litigation related to accessibility for individuals with disabilities has been extrapolated into accessibility for all students. For example, the use of closed captioning when watching videos is no longer an option for educators—it is a requirement. Educators must embrace accessibility so as not to identify students with disabilities or teach to the exception. The use of closed captioning may prove useful for students taking some classwork online.

Much like the utilitarian philosophical perspective, where the emphasis is on the greater good, UDL embraces the idea that learning is about the greatest number of people (students) having access to information without asking for accommodation; it is *proactive*, not *reactive*. Identifying UDL as a "plus-one mind-set" means educators prioritize "one more way that you can help keep learners on task, just one more way that you could give information, just one more way that they could demonstrate skills."[15]

In a higher-educational culture of assessment, educators ask questions about the effectiveness of their course materials and try to be proactive in problem solving. For example, is there a place in the course where students always have questions? Might you add one more option for students to learn that material, whether a video, website, or extra readings? UDL brings proactive teaching front and center for achieving course outcomes and can empower Gen-Z. UDL models and identifies perspective taking and critical thinking before stumbling blocks arise. In a way, teachers take out their own snowplows and work to clear paths for learning.

Adversity

We know that superheroes often face adversity in both their real and super-hero worlds. Gen-Zers, much like millennials, experience heightened levels of stress, anxiety, and depression. When students are in an educational set-ting, they can sometimes freeze or become incapacitated in their learning. Teachers who can appropriately recognize when students are experiencing one of these emotions may be able to better modify those experiences in positive ways.

Many Gen-Zers have also been classified in a broader sense as insecure. As noted earlier and also by Jean Twenge, author of *iGen: Why Today's Super-Connected Kids Are Growing Up Less Rebellious, More Tolerant, Less Happy—and Completely Unprepared for Adulthood*, the double-identity characteristic of Gen-Zers contribute to some of their anxiety, stress, and de-pression. Additionally, Twenge also states that "in the age of FOMO, teens are also likely say that they often feel left out," which can feed their anxiety and depression and may slow the development of intrinsic motivation neces-sary for learning.[16]

One step that teachers can take toward helping students face adversity is by building classroom climates that encourage students to take risks and sup-port each other when sharing information or ideas. For example, students often need to be reminded that there is no such thing as a dumb question. If a question is perceived by others, including the teacher, as dumb, then the chances of that student asking other questions or offering insights is greatly reduced. Instead, taking the question seriously and working through it with the class as a problem-solving exercise may benefit Gen-Zers more than simply saying, "That's a dumb question." It may mean repeating some course information in new ways or with new examples, but the goal here is to achieve learning outcomes. Reiteration of material is "one more way" to be effective in instruction.

Despite feeling that they belong to a comfortable classroom climate, many students, especially those with physical, emotional, cognitive, and other disabilities and those in a marginalized group (based on race, class, gender, sexuality, or ethnicity) continue to experience adversity. Educators need to be keenly aware of differences and work to improve their own perceived weaknesses of students. Educators can be role models by removing personal biases within the classroom. This is not an easy task and requires much reflexivity (thinking about what you are thinking and doing), practice, and patience, but it can support many students as they experience adversity and is another way to reach Gen-Zers.

Furthermore, educators might also encourage critical thinking, where all students have an opportunity to consider others' perspectives and emotions and make valued and credible arguments for and against a position or ideology. Probing students to answer the why, what, and how of such positions models critical thinking and engaged discourse based on factual information, not opinion. The adversity that some Gen-Zers face based on their personal views can be lessened when they can receive others' perspectives and adequately articulate their own. This also better prepares these individuals for a diverse workplace environment, as they become more competent and ethical communicators through this process.

Fallibility

All superheroes are fallible. They make mistakes or are unsuccessful in different ways. What is important for these superheroes is how they manage their own fallibility so that it doesn't lead to assumed or real failure within their lives. Gen-Zers want to please others and seek praise from those in authoritative roles. *How* educators respond to missed or late work is important, as many Gen-Zers haven't been properly conditioned that fallibility comes with consequences that may not feel good.

Because many of their parents have bought bigger and wider snowplows to pave the way (think John Deere big) than the parents of their millennial counterparts, consequences are not typically a primary concern for Gen-Zers. For example, missing an assignment isn't catastrophic because their parents, guardians, or teachers have always allowed them to turn something in beyond a deadline. Many parents have used their snowplows to clear a path for submission of late assignments by e-mailing, phoning, texting, and meeting with teachers to explain why they were late. Imagine the feelings of uneasiness that emerge when one educator or employer holds Gen-Zers to stated deadlines and turns the snowplow parent or guardian away.

Because Gen-Zers have not had to regularly manage these situations, their stress and anxiety increase, and their fallibility is more obvious. Greg

Lukianofff and Jonathan Haidt made this clear in their discussion of Gen-Z's ability to think rationally and make good decisions.[17] Some parents or guardians go up the ranks to have their children's work submitted and accepted, but educators need to learn to hold steady and impose the proper consequences for students. Allowing one student to hand in a late assignment with no penalty sets precedent for other students in the class.

One way to emphasize the seriousness of students' wayward choices for assignments is to have a clearly written policy for each assignment and *stick to* that policy. Can students earn partial credit for missed or late assignments? Be specific about the consequences. Is it a grade deduction on the final grade of the assignment for each twenty-four-hour period that passes? If so, then say so! Students cannot be given carte blanche to do as they want when there are others involved. The integrity of the instructor is on the line.

Gen-Zers also experience fallibility with a sensitivity to offensive speech, especially against marginalized groups. As individuals get older, they find out that not everyone holds the same perspectives about social justice issues. When negative claims about marginalized groups are presented in their educational settings or local communities, Gen-Zers often take personal offense. In trying to better align with the struggles of marginalized groups, Gen-Zers seek to *shut down* events, lectures, and speeches that violate their own personal sensibilities.

The challenge here is that the First Amendment of the US Constitution protects the rights of dissenting groups to speak and peacefully protest. Take a moment to reflect on recent protests where neither side really listens to the other, leading to heightened tempers. Such was the case during a 2017 march in Charlottesville, where the Unite the Right Rally was met by oppositional protests, leading to one rally participant driving a car into the oppositional crowd.[18] Oftentimes, how people present themselves (their identities) exacerbates the tensions between the conflict participants, even before the event takes place. Gen-Z must learn how to manage these moments and to accept (as best as possible) that people's ideologies are different.

Independence

To this point, one might be able to successfully argue that Gen-Zers pride themselves on being fiercely independent (sort of). They have been raised with access to free courses, videos, websites, podcasts, and more that provide information and the know-how on any imaginable topic at the click of a mouse button. It is true that Gen-Zers prefer to work alone and at their own pace; however, there lies the conundrum: They also desire copious amounts of feedback.

While these individuals prefer independent learning, they also enjoy working in group settings that share a common physical space but are allowed to still primarily focus on their individual devices.[19] Gen-Zers identify this as social learning, and it is often exhibited by group members sitting next to each other, like birds on a wire. This environment allows them to solve problems that arise during the assignment but also invokes a call to creativity, which they seem to embrace when learning.

In summary, Vivek Pandit, Gen-Zer and author of *We Are Generation Z: How Identity, Attitudes, and Perspectives Are Shaping Our Future*, says it best: "[T]he use of personal digital technology to study at one's own pace while receiving constant feedback" is paramount.[20] Perhaps the gamification of learning went a bit too far for millennials. However, the possibility of completing tasks, earning badges, and applying new knowledge to the real world may be just the place to begin when assisting students in developing and applying their intrinsic motivation inside the classroom. If Gen-Zers are willing to freely sign up for online courses, watch videos, and investigate other topics of interest in their free time, then educators must find ways to harness that willingness in the classroom—by making material and content relevant and accessible; perhaps even visual; and, somehow, individualized.

PERCEPTIONS OF GENERATION Z

Superheroes Unmasked

7

PERCEPTIONS OF
THESE SUPER BEINGS

"We are capable of so much more than we think we are. All we have to do is reach for it. All we have to be is fearless."
—*Captain Marvel*

We've made three major claims about Generation Z: First, we live in a world where superheroes have a heightened visibility within our cultural discourse. Second, not only are the ideas of superheroes increasingly prominent, but there are also organizations supporting real-world children in superhero contexts. Think Disney's *Marvel's Hero Project*, a series that follows kids making a difference across communities by dedicating their lives in selfless acts of bravery and kindness. As a result, featured children have their own individual Marvel comic created based on their personal story. Projects like these reinforce the superhero phenomenon and further lends itself to this research.

To reach our third claim, we conducted our own generational survey using Amazon Mechanical Turk (MTurk) and Qualtrics, collecting more than one thousand responses from representatives spanning five generations: traditionalists, baby boomers, Gen-Xers, millennials, and Gen-Zers. Responses were analyzed to better understand the perceptions of Gen-Z in relation to the six superhero characteristics. Responses from the survey translate directly to the third major claim about this generation, those qualities of Gen Zers: double identity, second job, fallibility, just causes, adversity, and independence. The outcome of this survey indicated that each of these superhero characteristics emerged as larger research themes.

RESEARCH DEMOGRAPHICS*

In total, 1,052 anonymous respondents completed the survey, each identifying within one of five generational cohorts: traditionalists (5), baby boomers (104), Gen-Xers (285), millennials (528), and Gen-Zers (130). In relation to gender, 619 respondents identified as female, 427 identified as male, and 6 respondents preferred not to answer. Of note, due to the minimal number of traditionalists who participated in the survey, much of the final reported data pertaining to the superhero characteristics may not include the traditionalists' responses.

By leveraging a tool such as Amazon MTurk, researchers can connect with respondents of all backgrounds. In this survey, respondents either identified as White/Caucasian (72.91 percent), Asian (11.20 percent), Black or African American (10.47 percent), American Indian (1.47 percent), Hawaiian Pacific Islander (0.46 percent), or other (3.49 percent).

When preparing the survey questions, we extended some demographic responses beyond the usual requested responses, especially because we claim that millennials and Gen-Zers tend to be more open to cultural differences in many social categories. For example, when inquiring about sexuality and sexual preference, categories included not only heterosexual (85.36 percent), bisexual (6.75 percent), and homosexual (3.52 percent) but also pansexual (1.81 percent), asexual (0.67 percent), other (0.19 percent), and prefer not to say (1.71 percent). A deeper dive into the data indicates that Gen-Xers, millennials, and Gen-Zers tend to expand their response options more than the two older generations. In fact, no traditionalists or baby boomers indicated pansexual, asexual, or other in this question. This most likely reflects the generational-based core beliefs discussed previously, indicating

---

*This research was conducted prior to COVID-19. Therefore, the impact of the pandemic is not reflected in the responses to this survey.

that that these two generations may be more likely to comply with social norms for sex, gender, and sexuality.

Available responses related to religious affiliation were also expanded. Christianity tended to dominate, with unspecified Christians (300), Catholics (177), and Protestants (115) making up slightly more than half of the total respondents. An additional 384 survey respondents selected the "none" category for this topic. On the surface, this makes sense because millennials have been identified as one of the first generations to either embrace no formal religion or express their spirituality in more personal, private ways. Just over one-third (36.50 percent) of all respondents reported no religious affiliation, while the second-highest identified religion among all generations was unspecified Christianity (28.5 percent). Given that all Christian religions and "nones" accounted for 92.78 percent of survey responses, responses from people who follow Eastern religions or other spiritual paths is limited. The number of individuals claiming no religious affiliation may continue to increase as Gen-Zers mature.

Moreover, political party identification choices included not only Democratic (435) and Republican (284) but also Independent (220) and none (110) (3 respondents chose not to answer this question). So, while more than half of total respondents (68.3 percent) identified with traditional US political parties overall, nearly one-third did not, as Independents (20.9 percent) doubled the number of respondents with no political affiliation (10.5 percent). Interestingly enough, the number of individuals identifying most closely as Democratic increased the farther they were removed from the traditionalist generation: 0 percent of traditionalists, 26 percent of baby boomers, 37.2 percent of Gen-Xers, 44.3 percent of millennials, and 52.3 percent of Gen-Zers. We noted this shift toward increasingly Democratic underpinnings for millennials in our previous book, *The Millennial Mindset*, for which the trend seems to continue with Gen-Zers.

A further breakdown of political demographics from the survey indicated that 922 individuals declared themselves registered voters, with 110 not registered and 20 unsure about their voter-registration status. A generational breakdown of voter registration paints an interesting picture of decreasing voter participation as the generations move closer to Gen-Z: Traditionalists reported 100 percent voter registration; baby boomers, 97.1 percent; Gen-Xers, 93.3 percent; millennials, 85.8 percent; and Gen-Zers, 74.6 percent.

This data affirms prior claims regarding the voting records of younger generations, which are lowest among all other voting-age generations. So, while millennials and Gen-Zers will dominate the workplace in a few years, they do not seem nearly as interested in voting or registering to vote as other generational cohorts—somewhat at odds with their interest in fighting for just causes and facing adversity. Perhaps, their high levels of anxiety play a role in this data?

TECHNOLOGY USE

Regarding technology, respondents were asked to identify each of the devices they used. From this data, our assumptions about technology use were largely confirmed when laptops (895) and tablets (554) were the most widely used devices, both of which are mobile and appear to support the 24/7 digiverse that all generations experience in today's world. Surprisingly, desktops yielded 528 responses, and although not mobile by nature, they provide an outlet for many generational cohorts to participate in the digiverse. With all the available options related to images, printers were also used quite frequently (553), most regularly by baby boomers (76.9 percent) and Gen-Xers (61.8 percent). So, who is using these other devices? Which generations are drawn to which technologies?

- Traditionalists preferred to use laptops and desktop computers, with none reporting use of smartwatches, streaming devices, DVRs, e-readers, or tablets.
- Baby boomers were most comfortable using laptops, desktops, and tablets but also had experience with various other devices. They did, however, report that smartwatches and satellite radio were used the least.
- Gen-Xers favored laptops, followed by satellite radio, tablets, desktop computers, and HDTVs, with one individual reporting no ownership of any of these devices. Smartwatches had the lowest reported usage of all devices for this generation.
- Millennials preferred to use laptops, tablets, desktops, and streaming media devices but also reported the second-highest use of smartwatches of all generations (16.5 percent).

- Gen-Zers also favored laptops, desktops, and tablets, with minimal reported use of satellite radios, DVRs, e-readers, and GPS car-navigation systems. Gen-Z led all generations with the use of smartwatches (31.5 percent), nearly one-third of all respondents. One respondent reported no ownership of any of these devices, which is rare but understandable, given the smartphone's capabilities nowadays.

In terms of what activities were most frequently conducted while using these devices, online searching (839), video streaming (746), shopping (705), audio streaming (691), playing games (631), and posting to social media (600) were the most prominent responses. Generational data yielded the following:

- Traditionalists tended to search, shop, and manage money the most frequently while using their devices, while streaming or creation of any type of content and playing games were the least-reported activities.
- Baby boomers indicated they also search, shop, and manage money most often while using their devices, followed by streaming visual content and playing games (61.5 percent each). Notably, neither these baby boomers nor traditionalists engaged in online dating, which also reflects previous research and social norms.
- Gen-Xers engaged in searching, managing money, and shopping the most, followed closely by streaming content. Also, 9.8 percent of Gen-Xers reported authoring blog posts, higher than both baby boomers and traditionalists but lower than millennials and Gen-Zers. The least frequently reported activity was online dating (8.8 percent).
- Millennials reported searching, streaming of all types of content, and managing money as their frequent online activities. Members of this generation also reported authoring blog posts less often than their Gen-X counterparts (8.9 percent) but are also more active in online dating (12.9 percent).
- Gen-Zers indicated that searching, streaming content of all types, playing games, and shopping were the most frequent activities that they engaged in while on their devices, followed by managing money and posting to social media channels. Not surprisingly, Gen-Zers also engaged in more online dating than other generations (19.2 percent).

Interestingly, Gen-Zers do not report as much authoring of blog posts as Gen-Xers and millennials but do report the highest social media engagement of all generations (64.6 percent).

When asked to respond to questions related to turning off or powering down smartphones, 462 (43.96 percent) of all survey respondents said they *never* do this. Note that *only* 24 (2.28 percent) participants indicated that they did not have a smartphone. Other respondents turned off or powered down daily (14.75 percent), weekly (21.12 percent), two to three times a week (10.66 percent), and three to four times a week (7.23 percent). Generational data yielded the following results:

- Traditionalists: 100 percent have a smartphone
- Baby boomers: 5.8 percent do not have smartphones
- Gen-Xers: 2.5 percent do not have a smartphone
- Millennials: 2.1 percent do not have smartphones
- Gen-Zers: 100 percent have smartphones—not surprising!

The data suggests that regardless of generational cohort, most people have smartphones (97.7 percent). However, a closer analysis of the role of smartphones indicates that 43.9 percent of all respondents *never* turn off their phones, with 49.2 percent of Gen-Zers and 47 percent of millennials preferring never to turn off their phones. Incidentally, of the remaining 50.8 percent of Gen-Zers who do choose to turn off their phones, only 23.1 percent are most likely to do so once a week, which is still quite a high percentage for these digital natives. In fact, across survey respondents, the range of people who turn off their phone once a week fell between 18 and 23 percent.

Of those individuals choosing to power down their smartphones four to six times a week, millennials (8.14 percent) and Gen-Xers (7.39 percent) led the way. Others who indicated they turned off their smartphones slightly less frequently, two to three times a week, were also led by millennials (11.93 percent), with Gen-Xers (10.21 percent), baby boomers (9.62 percent), and Gen-Zers (4.62 percent) closely behind. Respondents noting that they only turn off their smartphones once a week were most often Gen-Zers (23.08 percent), followed by Gen-Xers (21.48 percent), millennials (21.02 percent), traditionalists (20 percent), and baby boomers (18.27

percent).* The data suggests that Gen-Zers could be considered the generation least likely to turn off their phones—and if they do, it is fewer times a week—further supporting claims made in previous chapters about this generation being digital natives and perceived as addicted to their smartphones.

Additionally, in an effort to provide insights into the role that a smartphone plays in their daily lives, respondents were asked about the individuals whom they communicate with and the level of importance that these relationships hold in different contexts. The survey results indicated that when it comes to communicating with others, such as family, friends, or coworkers, social media platforms provide more opportunities for outreach for Gen-Xers, millennials, and Gen-Zers and less outreach for previous generations.

With so many social media platforms, texting, e-mails, and other ways to connect in the moment, immediacy did not quite fit into any one characteristic. Instead, immediacy is reflective of digital natives who face adversity, fight for just causes, and want solutions *now*. This may lead to impatience, which can then increase their opportunities for fallibility and compromise their independence. What we do know thus far is that while Gen-Z is capable of communicating with a variety of audiences, they are often perceived as not working well with others, requiring much feedback and direction, and not fully using critical-thinking skills to find solutions on their own. Couple this with the perception that Gen-Z is the most difficult generation to interact with (31.68 percent), followed by baby boomers (26.36 percent), millennials (17.22 percent), traditionalists (16.46 percent), and Gen-Xers (8.28 percent), we assert that Gen-Z has a lot of work to do in convincing others of their positive characteristics.

RESEARCH THEMES: SUPERHERO CHARACTERISTICS

The research revealed several themes that connected back to the superhero characteristics.

---

* This data represents responses from the individual generational cohorts and is not intended to represent the entire population. Therefore, 23 percent of Gen-Zers (out of all Gen-Zers) turn off their phones once per week, and 21.5 percent of all Gen-Xers turn off their phones, and so on throughout the remainder of the generations. This presentation of data is not intended to be additive; rather it represents the percentage of responses from each generational cohort.

Double Identity

As highlighted throughout this book, Gen-Zers were born into the digi-verse. They are a generation, much like millennials, that must balance both their real and online lives when clear boundaries between the two may not be obvious or even desired. When respondents were asked to identify the characteristics that they most associated with Gen-Zers, traits related to the digiverse were attributed most frequently. Of note, Gen-Zers are most commonly classified as or associated with being addicted to their smartphones (62.2 percent), digital natives (59.6 percent), desiring mobile access (53.4 percent), and possessing multiple identities (51.7 percent). Survey respondents also identified Gen-Zers' need for immediacy (45 percent) and communicating using images (40.4 percent).

The Internet and social media platforms are invasively prominent in the lives of Gen-Zers, so it makes sense that other generations might associate digiverse characteristics with Gen-Z. In addition, when evaluating Gen-Z's multiple identities, Gen-Zers stood above the rest (61.5 percent), followed by millennials (52.7 percent); however, baby boomers (44.2 percent) and Gen-Xers (48.1 percent) did not identify multiple identities as prominently for Gen-Zers. It is possible that these two generations may not think about online identity when interpreting this question.

As noted previously, some of the more common phrases identified by the survey included *addicted to smartphones, desired mobile access, digital natives*, and *communicated with images*. The outcomes for these categories are presented here:

- Survey respondents indicated that Gen-Zers were addicted to their smartphones, but Gen-Zers themselves were the least likely to confirm this as true, with 58.5 percent of this generation selecting this response. This was followed closely by millennials (59.3 percent). The perception about Gen-Zers' addiction to smartphones steadily increased with the remaining generations: 63.5 percent of Gen-Xers and 76.9 percent of baby boomers associated Gen-Zers with this trait. These results are most likely influenced by the presence of smartphones in Gen-Zers' lives and in media-related images and advertising.

- Baby boomers (60.6 percent) most frequently indicated that Gen-Zers desired mobile access. Surprisingly, Gen-Zers self-reported at 59.2 percent, which was lower than we expected with the prominence of apps like Uber, DoorDash, Grubhub, and more. Two of the remaining generations, Gen-Xers (53 percent) and millennials (50.6 percent), identified this trait with Gen-Zers less often. So, while the two older generations perceive Gen-Z as desiring mobile access, the three younger generations did not identify this descriptor nearly as frequently, with Gen-Zers reporting this descriptor least. Interestingly, less than two-thirds of Gen-Zers report that they *don't* desire mobile access as much as others believe they do.
- Gen-Zers self-reported being digital natives the most (62.3 percent), with Gen-Xers (61.1 percent), millennials (58.3 percent), and baby boomers (58.7 percent) reporting this descriptor less prominently.
- Part of being a digital native is having a social media presence. As a result, Gen-Zers attempt to become influencers on the social sphere. Their real-world lives meld with their online presence, thus creating the double identity. Gen-Zers overwhelmingly associated themselves with the term *influencer* (53 percent), with millennials a distant second (30 percent). Any other generations failed to garner a 20 percent association with this term.
- Some survey respondents indicated that Gen-Zers communicate using images, the last descriptor associated with double identity in the survey, but Gen-Zers self-reported that characteristic less than half the time (49.2 percent), while baby boomers (46.2 percent), millennials (38.4 percent), and Gen-Xers (37.5 percent) followed further behind. This descriptor does not appear to be a clear indicator of their double identity, as all generations associate this trait with Gen-Z less than 50 percent of the time.

Though double identity is a noted superhero characteristic, many of the descriptors of double identity were not associated with Gen-Z as often as we initially thought. The duality of living one's actual life while also living single or multiple lives online is at the center of Gen-Zers' existence in a multitude of other ways. These superheroes operate in a binary universe, where their two identities complement one another because of their differences. Secret identities transform superheroes, just as dual identities transform and influence Gen-Zers.

Second Job

Gen-Zers have a propensity to seek out employment options that allow for an above-average work-life balance, as well as provide the ability to pursue other outside interests that are deemed important (other jobs, volunteer opportunities, etc.). Leveraging their entrepreneurial spirit, Gen-Zers oftentimes identify opportunities at a young age. As a result, Gen-Zers rank highest in their desire for flexibility and pursuit of outside interests.

Not surprisingly, the desire to achieve a reasonable work-life balance, flex their entrepreneurial muscles, and know that they are not working to live are all important characteristics commonly associated with Gen-Zers. The survey results support these preferences as follows:

- When identifying the generation most widely associated with work-life balance, 32 percent of survey respondents aligned this trait most closely with members of Gen-Z, while millennials (26.9 percent), baby boomers (25 percent), and Gen-Xers (22.8 percent) trailed behind.
- When respondents were asked to indicate elements that contribute to an ideal work environment, 79 percent of Gen-Z respondents noted that flexible work hours were the most important component of a job. On average, this was approximately 10 percentage points higher in importance than for other generational respondents. Furthermore, employers looking to attract Gen-Z talent should take notice of the work amenities valued by this generation (games, food, events, etc.), with nearly 37 percent of Gen-Z respondents desiring these working arrangements. Millennials also indicated that these features contribute to a positive work environment (26 percent).
- Additionally, Gen-Zers are more closely associated with entrepreneurialism, nearly twice as often as their generational peers. Respondents indicate that Gen-Zers are the most entrepreneurial (46.9 percent), with millennials (29.4 percent) following a distant second and Gen-Xers, baby boomers, and traditionalists rounding out the results.

With Gen-Zers associated most commonly with entrepreneurialism and the pursuit of a reasonable work-life balance, one could conclude that members of this generation often seek flexible working arrangements in order to pursue their alternate interests.

Just Causes and Adversity

Generation Z has made its mark by explicitly voicing their stance on a variety of topics. By marching in the streets and standing up for social causes, Gen-Zers have become both activists and social justice heroes. They believe in what is right and are willing to work together for change. Whether tackling social, political, or environmental issues, Gen-Zers have shown that they are willing to take on adversity. Not surprisingly, survey results show all generations highly attribute just causes to Gen-Zers:

- Nearly half (45 percent) of all participants noted that activism was most closely associated with members of Gen-Z. The next-closest generational cohorts associated with activism was Gen-X and millennials (28 percent each). In fact, members of Gen-Z had nearly 20 percent higher participation over the past year in some form of social media (61 percent) or in-person activism (45 percent). Surprisingly, members of the baby boom generation were least likely to be associated with activism (13 percent), considering many within this cohort protested the Vietnam conflict.
- When discussing such issues as gender, sexuality, equality, and marriage, Gen-Zers embrace social justice at a higher rate (61 percent) than other generations. This speaks to the fact that Gen-Zers are associated with being more openminded about these topics (55 percent), with millennials trailing far behind (33 percent).

These results support much of what has been described throughout the book. While this generation may be plagued with such issues as climate change and various forms of inequality, Gen-Zers are tuned in and engaged to make positive changes within their communities. Much like a superhero, Gen-Zers face adversity head on and do not shy away from their beliefs.

Fallibility

One of the most oft-denied superhero characteristics among Gen-Zers is their fallibility. Few generational cohorts believe Gen-Zers are fallible. In earlier chapters, we discuss the rationale behind why we believe Gen-Z is fallible, whether they admit it or not. Survey respondents also noted how this characteristic was expressed by Gen-Zers: anxiety. Survey respondents identified *anxiety* (43.3 percent) as the most recognizable term associated with Gen-Zers' fallibility, along with *fragile* (32.4 percent), *depressed* (26.3 percent), and *fallible* itself (14.6 percent). The following are highlights from the survey:

- Gen-Zers showcased some self-awareness when associating themselves with anxiety (56.9 percent), followed by millennials (44.1 percent), baby boomers (38.5 percent), and Gen-Xers (37.2 percent). The generational perceptions of Gen-Zers as being less anxiety-filled than as perceived by Gen-Zers themselves may be a factor in how workplaces and educational settings meet the needs, or don't, of Gen-Zers in the coming years.
- Gen-Zers also led the way with reporting an association with depression (46.9 percent). Other generations reported their perception of Gen-Z as being depressed at a significantly lower rate, with millennials (26.1 percent) and Gen-Xers (19.6 percent) being the next-closest generational cohorts to associate that term with Gen-Zers. We believe these perceptual differences among generations will, and do, affect the expectations of Gen-Zers in the workplace and classroom because those who employ, work with, and teach Gen-Zers may not perceive depression in their younger counterparts. This may suggest that older generations have less patience and tolerance for depression or may even uphold their perceptions that Gen-Zers are isolated, do not work well with others, and are the most difficult generation to engage.
- Only one in five Gen-Zers (20 percent) correlate fragility with themselves, with baby boomers (35.6 percent), millennials (34.3 percent), and Gen-Xers (33 percent) describing them as fragile far more frequently. Again, these perceptual differences influence generational communication in the workplace and classroom and are something for all generations to consider when interacting with each other.

- As indicated previously, fallibility is considered a superhero character-istic. When it comes to perceptions of Gen-Zers as being fallible, sur-prisingly, Gen-Zers reported the lowest rate (7.7 percent), while other generations report about a 20 percent rate of frequency in associating Gen-Z with fallibility. The data suggest that Gen-Zers themselves are much less likely to consider themselves fallible. Their can-do attitude may be just the trigger for a level of concern from members of other generational cohorts in both the workplace and the classroom.

Additionally, survey respondents noted that Gen-Zers appear to need repeated direction and require more feedback. While Gen-Zers want to be independent, their need for repeated direction can lead others to view them as less capable—in both the classroom and the workplace. Subsequently, because members of this generation are already perceived as addicted to their smartphones, other generational cohorts view them as more isolated, not team-oriented, and not able to work well with others. In fact, Gen-Zers were noted to be the most difficult generation to work with by nearly one-third of all survey respondents. Of course, it was also Gen-Zers (34.6 percent) and millennials (33.7 percent) who noted that baby boomers were the most diffi-cult to engage. Generational perceptions indicate that older generations find the younger ones most difficult to engage, while younger generations find just the opposite. This could be why the negative phrase "Okay, Boomer" has emerged in our culture.

Independence

As described in *The Millennial Mindset*, one would be hard-pressed to find a generation that does not view itself as independent. When thinking about independence in relation to other descriptors used in the survey for this book, the following correlates with our understanding of independence most closely:

- One criticism of younger generations is that they do not have highly evolved critical-thinking skills. This aligns with the results of the survey, as millennials (17 percent), baby boomers (15.4 percent), and Gen-Xers (13.3 percent) were less prone to attribute critical-thinking skills to members of Gen-Z; however, Gen-Zers self-reported in a far more positive light when using this descriptor (43.8 percent). This suggests that Gen-Zers are three times as likely to associate themselves with a heightened aptitude for critical thinking. One implication of this finding is that the generations of individuals who raise, employ, work with, and teach Gen-Zers maintain the opposite perceptions when it comes to Gen-Zers and this skill.

- Gen-Zers associated with flexibility (not physical) nearly half of the time (49.2 percent). Not surprisingly, other generational counterparts reported this descriptor with less frequency, with baby boomers (24 percent), Gen-Xers (20 percent), and millennials (25.8 percent) viewing them as far less flexible. The implication for home settings, workplaces, and classrooms may be that Gen-Zers require much more structure, feedback, and guidance than they would personally admit to.

- Gen-Zers (39.2 percent) reported that they are more futuristic than any other generation. Millennials (27.1percent) associated this term with Gen-Zers the second-most frequently, with baby boomers (21.2 percent) and Gen-Xers (18.2 percent) trailing far behind. We believe that the high rate of responses for the perception of Gen-Z's need for immediacy may lead to the disparate responses for this descriptor.

- Prior and ongoing generational research indicates that Gen-Zers seek direct and unique feedback and interaction from a variety of influences within their lives, including brands, celebrities, athletes, organizations, individuals, and causes they may follow on social media. As a result, one might anticipate that other generations could perceive Gen-Zers as embracing customization. Gen-Zers did report the highest association with embracing customization (21.5 percent), followed by millennials (18.8 percent), Gen-Xers (14.7 percent), and baby boomers (7.7 percent). No traditionalists attributed this descriptor to members of Gen-Z.

Overall, the results from the survey support that most of the superhero characteristics are indeed attributed to Gen-Zers. What we have learned is that much more research and increasingly pointed questions need to be asked to delve deeper into these associations. We also recognize that intergenerational differences in perceptions of self and others are sometimes quite divergent, suggesting that improvements in communication between and among generations are necessary to increase productivity and success at home, in the workplace, and in the classroom. Will the next generation don a cape or wear a mask?

In the last chapter, we offer some insight into who the next generation, Generation Alpha—The Adaptables—could turn out to be. We already know that children just starting their early elementary journeys are experiencing a far different world than either millennials or Gen-Zers have. What those implications and differences are? Only time will tell.

PREPARING
SUPERHEROES

The Future

8

SUPREME GUIDANCE

Interacting with Gen-Z

"The fate of your planet rests not in the hands of gods. It rests in the hands of mortals."—Thor

Following a similar format used in our last book, there is great benefit in providing suggestions and guidance for interacting with members of Gen-Z. In this chapter we share our insights with parents, guardians, educators, coworkers, employers, and Gen-Zers themselves so that they understand how to interact with their own generational cohort as well as other generations, especially as they prepare for their futures.

In *The Millennial Mindset*, we outline six fact-or-fiction statements related to Gen-Z.[1] The following statements were derived from the characteristics attributed to millennials and are provided here to contextualize who we thought Gen-Zers would become as they matured:

1. Gen-Zers are the same as millennials.
2. Gen-Zers will be even more connected than millennials.
3. Gen-Zers will be contradistinctive.
4. Gen-Zers will be confident, cavalier, and committed change agents.

5. Gen-Zers still prefer a hands-off leadership style and will demand less collaboration.

6. A new *C*, *customization*, will emerge for Gen-Zers, and this will make them more contradistinctive than ever.[2]

Each statement is addressed here, with suggestions for interacting with and among Gen-Z.

GEN-ZERS ARE THE SAME AS MILLENNIALS.

We can say both emphatically *yes* and emphatically *no* to this statement. How can that be? Well, if you recall, the exactness of generational years' starts and stops are not fixed; rather, they are more fluid as they guide us in examining shifting patterns among generational cohorts. Many millennial characteristics are present in Gen-Z's homes, classrooms, and workplaces. As generations mature, they reflect some of the previous generations' characteristics but also branch out to find their own identities. The likenesses and differences between millennials and Gen-Z are captured by the responses to the following statements.

GEN-ZERS WILL BE EVEN MORE CONNECTED THAN MILLENNIALS.

Absolutely. As highlighted throughout the book, members of Gen-Z are truly digital natives who have never experienced a disconnect from the digital environment. However, their experience does not equal cognizance or awareness of that connectedness. For example, we can experience the death of a loved one but never recognize or be mindful of how that loss is currently affecting us. Today, the average age of children receiving their own smartphones is ten years old, down two years from the average age of millennials (twelve years old) when they received their first smartphones.[3] For those Gen-Zers who do not personally possess their own smartphones at an earlier age, a great majority have had access to others' devices since they were roughly two years old. Their use of these devices could come in the form of a timely distraction at a restaurant or when their parents needed their own time to disconnect. In addition to smartphones, Gen-Z children were exposed to modern technologies, such as artificial intelligence (AI) and virtual reality (VR), at earlier ages, too. From Alexa and Siri to Google and more, small children have learned from these AI bots and freely command the digiverse to complete tasks for them—all with the control of their voices. With the prevalence of the Internet and prominence of Wi-Fi, children are one click or voice command away from securing knowledge on any given topic—whether that information is accurate or not. This has many implications for parenting, teaching, and employing this generation.

GEN-ZERS WILL BE CONTRADISTINCTIVE.

Similar to millennials and other earlier generations, Gen-Z is contradistinctive. While it may ultimately only relate to the intensity of the trait, it is worth noting how they present as contradistinctive differently. The term *contradistinction* is defined as "distinction by opposition or contrast," and *contradistinctive* is the adjective form meaning "distinction made by contrasting the different qualities of two things."[4] Generations want to be distinct from past generations. In this case, the items compared are two generational cohorts' beliefs, values, behaviors, and attitudes. While the similarities between millennials and Gen-Z outweigh the number of absolute differences, the nuanced ways in which Gen-Z presents itself is key to identifying these differences.

As did most generations preceding them, Gen-Z seeks its own identity and desires to separate itself from prior generations, especially millennials. Both Gen-Z and millennials predominantly rely on smartphones and texts to communicate with friends, family, and others, with Gen-Z preferring texting as their primary mode of communication. In fact, the placement of the word *phone* after *smart* is ironic for Gen-Z, who really do not need or want the actual phone service. Gen-Zers want access to cell service and free Wi-Fi to make texting others more convenient and efficient. They will text rather than e-mail their friends and family, and if acceptable, they will do so in the classroom with their teachers and in the workplace with their coworkers and employers. Nowadays, most Gen-Zers do not actually know their friends' phone numbers; instead, they rely on the smartphone to retain that information once it is entered into their contacts. If a phone is "dead," then Gen-Zers are not able to use other people's phones to call those family members and friends because phone numbers are no longer memorized.

Free is another difference between these two generations. Gen-Z is always searching for the cheapest product or service. One could argue that their motto is "free is good." For members of this generation, many public spaces provide free access to basic Wi-Fi services, which is a necessary part of Gen-Zers' communicative world. The need for charging stations is also heightened for this generation. Colleges, libraries, airports, and other public and private locations have begun placing more charging stations in their environments to ensure people *stay* there rather than leaving to find a place to charge their devices. Some public libraries have even expanded their Wi-Fi services to local parks, so those individuals enjoying the outdoors also get free connectivity. Every generation wants to be different, and although the difference may be slight, it is distinct.

GEN-ZERS WILL BE CONFIDENT, CAVALIER, AND COMMITTED CHANGE AGENTS.

This statement is also far more fact than fiction. With numerous technological platforms at their beck and call, Gen-Zers gain confidence in their ability to create content on various social media platforms, in chat rooms, and on their personal blogs or podcasts. The ability to share their ideas with others, build a following, and go viral provides what pop culture artist Andy Warhol called "fifteen minutes of fame." Many Gen-Zers want to be influencers or online celebrities or even have their own video channels when they grow up—or even right now. They may strive to make a living online rather than in person. For example, Fiona Frills and Haley Pham are two YouTube influencers widely recognizable to those under twenty-four years of age.[5] Gen-Zers are not looking to just get by in life; they are looking to forge their own paths and often try to take control of the snowplow moving forward, which may not always be successful. However, this entrepreneurial spirit can benefit Gen-Z in the classroom, as well.

Because educators often use grades as performance indicators, Gen-Z may be risk averse in school. However, for Gen-Zers, it is the possibility of success via likes, followers, and sponsors that encourages them to take risks in the digiverse. They, too, serve as our digital foot soldiers on the front lines of the digitally connected world. Gen-Zers are the ones who try new technologies; use current technologies; and may even create new technologies, products, or services and will need to be ready to take over the workplace in the not-so-distant future. Educators can leverage this entrepreneurial spirit and reflect it within their curricula. Gen-Zers see people their age snowplowing their own paths and may begin to want to lead change rather than simply "like" that change in the digiverse.

The claim that Gen-Zers are committed change agents is *somewhat* accurate. Gen-Zers have moved from being solely hashtag activists, like most millennials, to also being in-person activists. For example, survivors of the 2018 Marjorie Stoneman Douglas High School shooting immediately organized events against gun violence. They used their experiences to try to create change, yet little policy change has occurred, gun violence is still prominent in the United States. Many Gen-Zers' commitment to this cause has slowed—that is, until the next mass school shooting occurs. This is not a criticism of Gen-Zers alone, as people tend to temporarily commit to acts of activism until more important life matters take precedence. However, there are some prominent activists with their own organizations still doing great work via their advocacy, including Greta Thunberg and Jamie Margolin, both climate change activists; Meltem Avcil, an activist fighting for refugee rights; Lili Evans, a body image activist; Jamie Sweeney and Nick Batley, male feminists trying to change the patriarchy; and Thomas Ponce, an animal rights activist.[6] There are also many Gen-Zers making their own marks in venture capitalism and elsewhere, thereby being exemplars of commitment. One example is Tiffany Zhong:

> As an 18-year-old, Tiffany Zhong was recognized as one of the leading teenage analysts for Binary Capitalists. She was also a venture capitalist herself and invested in multiple startups, becoming known as the world's youngest VC. Now in her early 20s, Zhong is an entrepreneur and self-proclaimed "teen whisperer." She serves as the bridge between Gen-Z and tech companies that are attempting to create Gen Z–focused apps and other tech.[7]

And then there is Shaivi Shah: "The fifteen-year-old who donated more than 150 hygiene kits to the homeless during the COVID-19 pandemic. She recruited classmates from her high school to make kits that included hand sanitizer, antibacterial soap, lotion and reusable masks."[8] They distributed these kits to help people experiencing homelessness during the pandemic. The rationale behind the commitment resulted from her fear that these individuals would be forgotten while people focused on their own families staying healthy and safe.

Finally, we have Genesis Butler: At three years old she became a vegetarian, by seven a public advocate for a vegan lifestyle, and by ten a TEDx speaker, bridging the worlds of environmentalism and animal consumption. Now, at 13 she is still making inroads in raising awareness and changing the world.[9] With access to information at their fingertips through a variety of platforms, Gen-Zers are capable and primed to set their own paths early in life.

GEN-ZERS STILL PREFER A HANDS-OFF LEADERSHIP STYLE AND WILL DEMAND LESS COLLABORATION.

Armed with a highly motivated entrepreneurial spirit, Gen-Z is looking to be its own boss and pave its own route to educational and financial success. An early 2019 survey by *Entrepreneurial* magazine finds, "Members of Gen Z seem to have lofty goals: Nearly one in four plans to personally bankroll their college tuition. About 41 percent plan to become entrepreneurs. And almost half believe they will invent something that changes the world."[10] Some success stories include many who open businesses, both for and not-for-profit, such as Jesse Kay, a "high schooler, podcaster, speaker, and entrepreneur from New Jersey. Jesse started his first business in 2009 at nine years old flipping shoes on eBay."[11]

Another example is Noa Mintz, founder of Nannies by Noa, a leading nanny placement service based in New York City. With its large network of highly experienced sitters and nannies with a passion for children, Nannies by Noa is the leading destination for reliable, engaging, and educated childcare providers.[12] And then, there is Maayan, a middle-schooler and developer of Queeng, a new deck of playing cards where the queen isn't worth less than the king—changing gender stereotypes and blasting masculine norms.[13] These entrepreneurs differ from millennials, who often resorted to side gigs to make a living; now, it is full gigs that take precedence. Even though these eighteen-to-twenty-four-year-olds had intentions greater than successful entrepreneurial realization, their futures are bright, and they strive for success.[14]

Gen-Zers also prefer to physically be near others when working on projects, but they want to work *individually* on these projects. Additionally, much like their millennial counterparts, they demand a heightened level of recognition and feedback on their individual contributions. They may not directly ask for feedback (or even know how to do so) from coworkers and employers, but they do indeed desire that feedback, especially when accolades may come their way. Their motivation to work hard is fueled by positive feedback.

A NEW *C*, *CUSTOMIZATION*, WILL EMERGE FOR GEN-ZERS, AND THIS WILL MAKE THEM MORE CONTRADISTINCTIVE THAN EVER.

Gen-Zers have been raised to showcase their purchasing preferences on an individual basis. No longer do they have to visit the local mall to get what they want. They have quickly become masters of comparison shopping, "try things on" in virtual dressing rooms, and even use services that allow them to rent or buy clothes selected specifically for them. Gen-Zers often stay home and have food delivered via Uber Eats, Grubhub, DoorDash, and other delivery services. They use ride-sharing services Uber and Lyft and can be certain of the prices ahead of time, unlike taxi services. Members of this generation also stream music, podcasts, movies, books, and more to their smartphones, tablets, laptops, and desktops when they want them.

The interconnectivity to these technological services is the key to their contradistinctiveness as a generation: customization appears to have no bounds. Perhaps soon there will be Uber or Lyft for private and commercial flights, where the user says, "I need to fly from Seattle, Washington, to Nashville, Tennessee," and carriers vie for that fare. In Albany, New York, the Capital District Transportation Authority (CDTA) is piloting a customized ride-share program called FLEX On-Demand Transit; a customizable ride-share program, its service is limited to certain parts of the region during its introductory phase.[15]

Certainly, social media advertising is still the boon, and brand influencers have been effective in finding and using new products and services to share with everyone, including Gen-Zers. When an influencer touts a product, Gen-Z will follow. Think Kylie Jenner, an influencer with a massive social media following and her own cosmetics line, which she sold for more than $500 million. Then there is Cristiano Ronaldo, thirty-five, a millennial and European soccer star who holds sponsorships with Nike and other brands and also has 200+ million followers, many of whom are Gen-Zers.[16]

Jenner and Ronaldo already had a following, so the link to influencer was easy. But there is a plethora of unknowns who overnight become influencers and eventually turn that influence into money. Take, for example, Leo Kelly also known on Instagram as "Shirley Temple King." After *People* food editor Shay Spence shared his discovery of Leo on Twitter, the six-year-old became an overnight sensation, with his following ballooning to nearly 270,000. He has appeared on such television shows as *Ellen* and signed on with United Talent to help promote his identity nationally. While marketers need to develop more organic partnerships with Gen-Z to have their products or services thrive in a customization economy, it is the entrepreneurial prowess in a digital world that truly sets Gen-Z apart from millennials and other generations.

In summary, the predictions that we made regarding Gen-Z nearly a half-decade ago were on target but not exact. With that, let's shift gears and provide specific suggestions and guidelines for parenting, teaching, and working alongside Gen-Z.

PARENTING GEN-Z

Acknowledge Your Own Generational Biases, Strengths, and Weaknesses

Too often, we make our way into the digiverse and search for information without much thought about whether what is delivered is fact or fiction. We share our beliefs, values, and attitudes at home and in public, especially via social media platforms. Parents or guardians must proactively acknowledge their own biases, strengths, and weaknesses because children learn from them daily.

We can, and should, model moments of reflection when we catch ourselves using stereotypes (e.g., boys will be boys) or making behavioral choices that may implicate our prejudices (e.g., clutching a purse tighter when people of a particular race approach). Parents and guardians should also recognize how their childhood was different from both their own parents' and their children's childhoods and acknowledge how these differences are not necessarily wrong or less important than their own. Placing importance on cultural change and assessing how or why that change may have occurred is the first step toward personal growth; diversity and difference should be appreciated, not denigrated.

Work on Your EQ (Emotional Intelligence)

Road rage, cyberbullying, and ghosting illustrate our inability to monitor our own and others' emotions. Perspective taking is a challenge for Gen-Zers, but the digiverse may be lessening previous generations' perspective-taking abilities, as well. We live in a world where participants in the digiverse can isolate themselves on websites and social media platforms in what has been called "echo chambers." Echo chambers are public and private spaces that only support *our* beliefs, values, attitudes, and behaviors and no others.[17]

These echo chambers can then filter into the real world; such is the case with the US Congress in 2020. Traditionalists, baby boomers, and Gen-Xers, who make up most congressional members, stooped to name calling and clear partisanship and even challenged others to playground fights. The United States also witnessed a presidential state-of-the-union address where partisan tensions reigned over the night; the leader of the House of Representatives ripped a copy of the speech in half at the close of the address, in full view of all spectators, whether online, via TV, or in person. This was *not* exemplary behavior and demonstrates a lack of emotional intelligence. Daniel Goleman and Richard E. Boyatzis's article and HelpGuide's EQ resource should prove helpful.[18] Practicing mindfulness techniques and improving emotional intelligence should be primary in our lives so positive role models emerge, especially via public figures.

Be Technological Role Models, Too:
Put Down Your Phones!

So often, parents or guardians claim that their children are addicted to their smartphones or other technologies without realizing that they are engaging in the same behavior. Having tech-free times with children can improve the quality of those relationships and model the importance of being present and connected to those we enjoy spending time with. Many have found this to be true during the pauses, stay-at-home orders, and quarantines experienced during the COVID-19 pandemic of 2020. Clearly, engaging in interpersonal communication with Gen-Zers and others will better prepare them for their futures, too.

Set Guidelines for Social Media

Regarding social media, it is important to establish clear social media and technology guidelines and policies. Discussions with your elementary-, middle school–, and high school–aged children about which social media they currently use, want to use, and can use and then setting limits on how often they can use their devices and why those restrictions are in place are great ways to begin. More and more frequently, students are asked by their teachers to use their smart technologies to complete their homework. Be sure to understand the school's expectations when creating these policies, as well. However, setting boundaries can also mean limiting your own time with these same smart technologies.

Once rules and expectations have been established regarding technological use within the home, it is also important to monitor use and enforce consequences for violations. Parents and guardians often determine the consequences, such as taking away a device for a specified amount of time. However, parents should also be willing to abide by those same rules and consequences, even though they are in charge; they are the role models here. Try to avoid a laissez-faire approach to a child's social media activity. Instead, peruse social media platforms and know about a child's accounts to monitor activity that may be detrimental to their identities, personal growth, and lives. This discussion has been around since the advent of the Internet. Today, parents need to be more vigilant than ever and monitor their own online identities and behaviors, as well, because they, too, can experience negative consequences.

Assess Ongoing Technology Use

In most instances, it would be irresponsible to solely rely on your own personal intuition about the impact of technology on society. Leverage your local library databases or Google Scholar to research the advantages and disadvantages of your children's and your own technology use. This information can allow you to make more informed decisions on your children's ages, maturity, and circumstances. The bibliography included at the end of this book identifies additional applicable resources.

Enforce Consequences for Bad Behavior

Whether you like it or not, we live in an era where our world leaders are in the spotlight, some by choice and others by virtue of their presence within the digiverse. As citizens, we are exposed to more information daily than ever before. World leaders may have said the wrong things, behaved inappropriately, tweeted inaccuracies, or even engaged in public name calling for all citizens to see and share. However, many of our world leaders do not necessarily suffer the consequences of these choices, and the repercussions are troublesome.

Think of US president Donald Trump. Countless examples of his behavior and communications have been lauded as poorly timed, misaligned, or distasteful or even have directly singled out specific groups or individuals. Parents and guardians can use these moments as examples for their own children, who may have to make decisions that may directly affect others. President Trump may ultimately receive a few moments of bad press, but his behaviors and tactics for communicating result in zero consequences to him in his role as president. This precedent at national and world levels encourages some people, especially younger ones, to engage in speech or behaviors that mock or hurt others. As a result, they, too, may expect zero consequences. One message is clear: The people with the most power win, with no costs to their standing or status. Accepting such behavior can inspire harassment of others.

Explain and Discourage Bullying

It is often difficult to believe that in our ever-evolving civilized communities, bullying is still prevalent, despite ongoing efforts at local, regional, and federal levels to slow its progress or end it once and for all. Whether classified as overt or disguised, intentional or unintentional, bullying is a problem. Parents and guardians must explain bullying in its simplest terms and then point out examples as they occur at home, in the classroom, or in the workplace. Three valuable resources are StopBullying.gov, the American Institutes for Research, and Workplace Bullying Institute.[19]

Minimize Coddling

Parents need to consider the distinction between when coddling might be appropriate and when it is done out of fear of hurting the child's self-esteem. Unnecessary or excessive coddling over time and throughout children's lives does not properly prepare them to manage disappointment, frustration, or failure.

For example, coddling is necessary when someone is grieving the loss of a loved one but is not always necessary when a child fails a test. Empathy and sympathy are certainly fitting in this instance, but taking it a step further and demanding that a teacher change the child's grade is easily snowplowing and coddling at its worst. Instead, it is important to teach children that it is perfectly okay to fail and to learn from their disappointments. As a parent, discuss the test itself and the studying process used, and assist the child in working differently on future tests. Even Elon Musk, CEO of Tesla, has experienced failure, but he also assumes failure is part of entrepreneurial ventures. He notes, "[F]ailure has a harmfully negative connotation. It appears failing at something means doing something wrong, or not being good enough. While at times that may be true, failure is also a part of the journey to success."[20] Parents or guardians should help children manage failure better and teach them how to respond to experiences in general.

Accept the Views of Others

One important topic to discuss with Gen-Zers is the idea that free speech does not mean only speech that reflects *your own* beliefs and values. Help

Gen-Zers accept the differences in views when someone's opinion does not align with their ideology. Children need to learn not to become physically and emotionally charged but to use an intellectual approach that invites civic discourse and perspective taking. While not an easy task, even for adults, Gen-Zers will benefit for years to come. In doing so, perhaps they can lessen the current partisan divide that exists today in the United States.

Promote Positive Discourse

Encourage Gen-Zers to speak up civilly to promote positive dialogue so their voices, and others', can be heard. Because Gen-Zers are more directly liberal or conservative in their political ideologies, their voices should not be silenced but used to improve democracy. Teach them how to constructively debate, take a stand, and create arguments based on the use of facts, not alternative ones, that have been verified from multiple and credible sources; teach them to be rational thinkers in those important moments.

Teach Life Skills

Beyond financial prowess, teach Gen-Zers to think more deeply about their beliefs, values, and behaviors, and others', too. Model critical thinking, fact checking, perspective taking, thinking outside the box, and patience every day. These should also be at the forefront in the classroom and workplace, as well.

One way to enhance life skills is to encourage Gen-Zers to focus on being present in the moment and not to scurry off to the next image, thought, or website. Their desire to get things done quickly (immediacy) in this fast-paced technological world does not mean they will make good choices or find accurate information. Help them use mindfulness tools to slow down, lessen their anxiety, and better their health. For assistance, try the Mindfulness website and Guided Mindfulness Meditation Practices with Jon Kabat-Zinn, and consider apps that may be more effective for Gen-Zers, such as Calm or Stop, Breathe, Think.[21]

Additionally, easy in principle and more challenging in practice is encouraging members of this generation to find answers on their own. When questions arise about homework or they are asked to do something by a coach or mentor, do not step in to do it for them. Have them problem solve first. If they are confused, help them talk the issue through with you. Nurturing and developing these skills will aid them in the classroom, workplace, and even in their personal relationships—but they *must* learn to think and work independently, not simply follow instructions.

EDUCATING GEN-Z

As educators we spend a large part of our day working with children of all ages. We have compiled a list of suggestions for educators to consider using in the classroom.

Teach Fact-Checking

We are living in an ever-popular fake news, alternative facts era. In fact, as of January 2020, the US president had made "more than 20,000 false or misleading claims" since taking office.[22] It is becoming increasingly difficult for anyone to truly decipher fact from fiction, and Gen-Zers are spending their formative years exposed to countless falsehoods on a daily basis. Now, many people, Gen-Zers included, realize that they can quickly locate answers or information by simply jumping into the digiverse. What many people do not realize is that speed of information is not as important as the quality and credibility of the information. It is imperative that educators, and others, too, assist Gen-Zers in identifying fact-checking resources. Otherwise, we may all be stuck in our "echo chambers" and not seek out alternative perspectives and truths. A couple helpful fact-checking resources are Politifact and FactCheck.org.[23]

Teach Ethics

In addition to the various political humiliations unfolding before them, Gen-Z has also witnessed cheating in multiple major league sports and other questionable behaviors during the first two decades of the twenty-first century. Ethical questions are front and center in Gen-Zers' lives, and they will need assistance from educators along the way to become more informed, media-literate, ethical citizens. Understanding different ethical philosophies, even at a basic level, can assist in making good decisions and much-needed perspective taking.

One of the most well-known examples used is a thought experiment called the trolley problem.[24] The problem looks something like this:

There is a runaway trolley barreling down the railway tracks. Ahead, on the tracks, there are five people tied up and unable to move. The trolley is headed straight for them. You are standing some distance off in the train yard, next to a lever. If you pull this lever, the trolley will switch to a different set of tracks. However, you notice that there is one person on the sidetrack. You have two options:

1. Do nothing and allow the trolley to take the lives of five people on the main track.
2. Pull the lever, diverting the trolley onto the sidetrack where it will take the life of only one person.

Which is the more ethical option? Or, more simply: What is the right thing to do?[25]

While there is debate about the efficacy of using this problem to teach ethics, it is an accessible and simple way to begin the discussion and encourages perspective taking. The National Education Association has a great website to get started.[26]

Work on Your EQ

Similar to how we addressed EQ with parents or guardians, we encourage increased awareness and improvement, as needed, in emotional intelligence for educators, as well. No matter how smart or technologically savvy they may be, educators may not be as adept in managing their own emotions or those of others.

In the early years of education, students' emotions run high and are displayed openly for all to see. As they get older, children learn to hide these emotions from their peers and elders in order to appear more mature. As an instructor, the more educated you are about EQ, the better chance you have in identifying subtle changes in students' behaviors and reading their non-verbal communication. Reaching out can prevent further deterioration of the mood, attitude, or behaviors in your classrooms and your students' lives. For starters, try Edutopia's "Emotional Intelligence: What Teachers Can Do."[27]

Draft Social Media and Technology Guidelines

Does your school have a social media policy? If you answered yes, then check to see if it includes staff and student policies specific to your classroom. If not, then you and your institution are far behind in guiding social media behaviors. If your institution does, then you are in relatively good shape and can shift focus toward determining whether it is acceptable to add to or alter those policies specific to the classroom. For example, you may find it useful to use the Kahoot app for in-class learning but only from tablets issued by the institution.[28]

Not only is it important to implement a general social media policy, but it is also helpful to have guidelines regarding personal tablet, laptop, and desktop use in the classroom and for assignments completed outside class. Think about what policies can be or currently are employed in your classroom. The idea is not to create a list of do-nots but rather to explain how you embrace technology and when its use is appropriate. Clear expectations of what is acceptable is needed for both transparency and a productive learning environment. If this classroom policy can incorporate student input, then it may be more effective. Remember, Gen-Z likes to share their opinions. If they help create the policy, then they will feel more vested in it.

When teaching Gen-Zers, consider including some of the following curricular and pedagogical suggestions:

- Employ more problem solving and less lecturing to create an engaging classroom. Allow Gen-Zers to take control and teach a lesson where they consider themselves *experts*. Have your students take an active role in their learning.
- Where possible, implement universal design. Create an "environment that can be accessed, understood and used to the greatest extent possible by all people regardless of their age, size, ability or disability."[29]

- Leverage technology. Enhance learning, beyond Google, to incorporate many forms of technology. But, if you have never used Google Voice, then perhaps it's time to try that out.
- Provide meaningful feedback to your students. If they missed the mark on an assignment, tell them why and how they can improve their work for the next assignment.
- Ask for feedback. Use exit tickets as quick evaluations of a lesson. Exit tickets are short (no more than two or three) questions asked at the end of a lesson to gauge what students understood. This not only helps students feel that their voice matters, but it also helps educators understand whether students learned what they needed to learn. Exit tickets can be used for short videos, online material (synchronous or asynchronous), group work, individual assignments, and lectures.
- Add virtual office hours. In addition to in-person meetings, leverage online and virtual office hours.
- Acknowledge that the "social learning" concept is at play for your Gen-Zers. Be specific about ways students can enhance their learning with study suggestions like Twitter Chats.
- Embrace the changing role of libraries and librarians at your institutions, especially when considering information literacy.
- Use connectivity tools like Zoom to hold classes in a virtual environment when appropriate, but beware the inherent dangers of doing so. During COVID-19, the phenomenon of Zoom bombing occurred. This is where an uninvited guest appears in an online gathering; disrupts the environment; or—worse—uses offensive remarks or images that are out of your control.

Engage in Professional Development

This generation looks at education considerably differently from previous generations and has a new attitude: one of being a customer. Their mind-set has changed and can be uncomfortable for educators. Keeping up with the educational research available in your discipline and grade level is important. Conferences, online or in-person classes, databases like ERIC, and your local library can provide up-to-date content and is generally only one search or click away.[30]

Keeping abreast of educational challenges and successes allows you to better assist your students' learning and keep your own teaching effective and relevant. Gen-Zers prefer educational assignments that apply directly to them. They also desire a combination of activities led by their teachers or professors, independence, experiential opportunities, and project-based learning assignments. Today's students keep educators on their toes. It is vital to stay current and understand the technology and how best to use it in the classroom.

WORKING ALONGSIDE GEN-Z

Acknowledge Personal Generational Biases, Strengths, and Weaknesses

As coworkers and employers, we sometimes forget that what we know about others is predetermined by our own experiences, values, and beliefs. We may not even realize just how rigid this knowledge is when interacting with others. For example, millennials fought to be noticed by other generational coworkers as valuable contributors in the workplace, and Gen-X attempted to stand out with baby-boomer managers. The same is true for Gen-Zers, who will struggle both with their own assumptions about other generations as well as what older generations think of them. In addition to generational differences, cultural and gender biases may need to be addressed.

Address Culture, Gender, and the Impact on Communication

While Gen-Z is often labeled the most accepting generation, their tolerance could also contribute to challenges within the workplace. Because people come from varying cultural backgrounds, their ideals sometimes conflict. For example, some baby boomers believe that men are more logical and organized than women, and that may contribute to whom they select to lead a project. Millennials may believe that Gen-Xers are technologically inept and unable to learn technology at their age.

What is helpful in these situations is to embrace diversity training as part of the company's infrastructure. Build in workshops, whether online or in person, for everyone at the organization—from top to bottom. Then, individually review materials on cultural differences based on your own immediate work environment. Becoming culturally aware of others is crucial to a successful and modern-day workplace. At long last, diversity, equity, and inclusion initiatives are becoming increasingly accepted in corporate America. Coworkers can

- research the advantages and disadvantages of continued and ongoing tech use;
- work on their own EQ; and
- look for reverse mentoring opportunities and employ open, dynamic leadership models.

Institute Workplace Social Media Policies

In many workplace environments, the use of social media is paramount in establishing and supporting relationships with clients. Be sure that coworkers and employees have work-related social media handles and accounts that are used to interact and connect with current and future customers. Professionalism is a must when creating handles; "Lustingforyou" or "NewEnglandPatriotsareTerrible" are not good work handles on any social media platform or work-related e-mail accounts.

Share and discuss social media policies immediately and frequently. If your organization does not have a policy, then you need to create one. If a social media policy does exist, then see when it was last updated, as social media platforms update frequently and may become increasingly or decreasingly relevant as the organization grows. What was created five years ago most likely requires revisions to meet the new platforms used today. Additionally, encourage the human resource team to hold focus groups related to social media practices, necessary for both the job and individual reasons. Perhaps simply allowing for two fifteen-minute social media breaks (one midmorning and one midafternoon) can alleviate the FOMO discussed in earlier chapters. Ensure that you also have clear guidelines for violations of the social media policy.

Be Flexible in the Workplace

As with millennials, Gen-Z is looking for flexibility in the workplace. Members of this generation desire to work remotely, either part time or full time, but it may also be beneficial to allow for flexibility in scheduling, if the type of work the organization engages in permits it. For example, if the marketing team is representing a shoe brand popular for younger millennials and adult Gen-Zers, then it might be useful to have flex hours for workers who can monitor social media sites late into the evening because these users are often on social media until the wee hours of the morning. However, if you are working on Wall Street, then working until the wee hours of the morning may not provide additional benefits beyond working normal business hours.

Additionally, the COVID-19 global pandemic introduced the world to the idea that many essential and nonessential businesses and their employees could effectively work remotely. In fact, employee productivity did not seem to fall during this unprecedented time in modern history. Gen-Zers lived through this pandemic and many will have attended school online. They may have seen their parents shift from office jobs to working remotely. Therefore, Gen-Zers will expect the ability for remote work as a viable option moving forward.

Provide Mentoring and Managing

As an employer, you must both manage and mentor Gen-Zers. This may sound silly, and you may be thinking, "Um, shouldn't we do that to all employees?" Well, yes, but this generation requires a keen balance between management and mentoring. Give lots of feedback. A frustration many coworkers and managers will face is the amount of feedback and clarity they will need to provide to Gen-Zers. Because the parents of this generation have explained or solved many of their problems, Gen-Zers tend to have issues working on their own or seeing a project through to completion when challenges arise. Continuous direction for assignments is encouraged.

As an employer or manager, you must cultivate independence and responsibility. As noted previously, neither of these traits necessarily come naturally to Gen-Zers. Kristen Fowler, a global executive for Clarke Caniff, a search firm, noted that a person directly out of college requires time to adjust to business expectations:

> [Y]ounger employees don't fully understand company needs and require management to play a large part in tying together both concept and expectations. . . . Many entering a new workforce environment create expectations of only working on tasks they enjoy. When this expectation is not met, they lose focus and, with computers and smartphones around, technology is typically the main distraction. Take the time to demonstrate the appropriate behavior for younger employees to follow. Doing so is a great step to building a strong work ethic.[31]

GENERATION-Z

What we have offered to this point are suggestions of how to better relate to or work with Gen-Zers. We recognize that the world does not—and should not—revolve around these individuals, and therefore we also provide a few tips for Gen-Zers to consider when interacting with members of other generational cohorts, so they, too, can take more responsibility for their actions.

Acknowledge Generational Biases, Strengths, and Weaknesses

Every generation brings its own unique qualities. Gen-Zers need to embrace others for these differences. You cannot simply dismiss others because you do not understand them or have never taken the time to get to know them. Developing your life skills is crucial in both your education and future employment. Acknowledge perceptual biases and work to improve on them. We suggest the following:

- Practice critical thinking by examining all the facts before making decisions.
- Know your audience. To whom are you speaking, texting, tweeting, and so on? Adjust your communication to the situation, person, and generational cohort.

- Familiarize yourself with your own verbal and nonverbal communication tics and styles. For example, make eye contact when communicating with others. This is a socially appropriate behavior and, for some of you, one that you must become comfortable with.
- Acknowledge cultural and gender differences and their impact on communication. Be sure to read up on how these differences influence perceptions during interactions.
- Employ a perspective-taking approach when interacting with others. Rather than thinking about yourself first, think of others and what they may be experiencing.
- Plan ahead by staying organized and knowing what's coming.
- Manage stress and anxiety in whatever way works best for you. This could be through exercise, meditation, food choices, or other options.

Work on Your EQ

Just as we have noted that others should develop and hone their EQs, so should you. Learning to manage your own emotions will help you communicate effectively, empathize with others, overcome obstacles, neutralize conflict with others, and generally become socially aware. When you understand and improve your own EQ, you are better able to maintain solid relationships with others and create productive environments. In a learning or work environment, you will be able to work on teams more effectively and better manage conflicts that arise. Your EQ relates directly to mindfulness—which is proven to be beneficial.

Be Present

Being present is crucial. With so many distractions—from text messages to alerts to checking social media—your generation struggles to be *in the moment* with anyone. Your attention span is approximately seven seconds, which means that your mind rapidly moves from one thought or idea to the next. Practice focusing your attention on what you are doing in the moment. Being mindful helps with this, aids your physical being, and helps you manage feelings. Ultimately, being mindful will help you become more self-aware.

Embrace Being Managed and Coached

Being managed can be one of the most difficult ideas to accept for Gen-Zers. Working on tasks that you do not consider fun or not part of the job description can cause you to become upset, stressed, and anxious. As an employee, reach out to your supervisor, and create daily, weekly, biweekly, or monthly touch-base meetings. Check in so that you know you are on track. These meetings can be an opportunity to learn where you are succeeding and where you need to focus more of your energy to be more productive.

Find Your Voice, and Become Independent

Educators and employers want to know they can trust you to work independently when given a task. Once you have your assignment, ask questions *in that moment*—not when the person walks away from you. Once you fully understand what is being asked of you, conduct your own initial research first. Do not rely on your teacher, manager, or coworker to explain *every* detail to you. Be independent; find answers first before you go back to ask clarifying questions.

CONCLUSION

Generation Z presents a multitude of both challenges and opportunities for us all. Like each previous generation, this cohort exhibits its own characteristics. Relationships with others are often atypical compared to previous generations. Their personalities can be multifaceted, their beliefs are strong, and they learn and process information differently from those who preceded them. By taking time to understand them, as well as ourselves, we can maximize their potential in life. We can do this, but we must do this together—and sincerely.

9

GENERATION ALPHA— THE ADAPTABLES

"Forget everything you think you know."—Dr. Strange

GENERATION ADAPTABLE

Shaped by such societal influences as Brexit, the COVID-19 global health pandemic, the widespread protests following the of the death of George Floyd, artificial intelligence (AI), and the dominance of smart devices, the next generation will feel the impact for years to come. As discussed early in the book, characteristics of each generation tend to be shaped by significant, defining historical events that take place during their formative years. Baby boomers, for example, lived through the Korean War and Vietnam conflict; Gen-Xers saw the Berlin Wall fall and civil rights rise; millennials experienced the 9/11 attacks; Gen-Zers saw heightened gun violence in schools; and this latest generation will have lived through a worldwide pandemic and the 2020 presidential election—the impact of which has yet to be fully realized.

Social researcher Mark McCrindle coined the name Generation Alpha in 2005 to identify those born between 2010 and 2024, the cohort following

Generation Z.[1] They are called Gen-Alpha and even sometimes referred to as "generation glass"—not because they will break but because of their early dependence on technology.[2] We have designated this cohort the Adaptables because they will have been forced to adjust to new conditions that prior generations (starting from traditionalists) did not experience. Adaptability as a skill refers to the capacity of people to change their actions, courses, or approaches to doing things in order to suit a new situation. The world changed overnight for this generation, so they had to adjust quickly to a new set of rules and social norms. These accommodations will forever influence the characteristics that define this generation and will ultimately prove to be long-lasting changes that occurred as a result of a significant moment in time.

Much of the early research about Gen-Alpha, or the Adaptables, was conducted prior to the COVID-19 global health pandemic and suggests that this generation will be even more technologically dependent than previous generations and that workplaces and classrooms will continue to change. As a result, some of the suggested characteristics surrounding this generation may not hold true once the Adaptables emerge from the pandemic.

For example, members of this generation currently enjoy various voice-oriented AI options to assist in their lives.[3] Therefore, we believe that it is quite possible that the COVID-19 pandemic may *increase* their desire for *real, in-person* human contact with actual friends, not AI beings like Siri, Alexa, or "Hey Google."[4] It is even plausible to think that the pandemic quarantine and self-isolation requirement may lead to screen fatigue. This could result in the Adaptables choosing prolonged human contact (at less than six feet away) rather than feeling compelled by some societal obligation or cultural norm. Their need for immediacy, however, just as with Gen-Z, in retrieving and creating messages via online and social media platforms will not allow them to completely disregard AI devices. It will, instead, require them to be more task oriented and information focused in leveraging these devices so they can obtain responses immediately.

The Adaptables, like Gen-Z, will continue to have multiple identities and hold a second job; they will face adversity in different forms; they will fight for just causes and increased economic equality; they will be fallible; and they, too, will be independent. But the notion of these characteristics being superhero-like may change. The Adaptables will have lived through the glorification of everyday champions. Essential employees, from frontline workers in grocery stores to transportation and facilities maintenance workers to doctors, nurses, respiratory therapists, pharmacists, and other healthcare personnel will take their place beside long-revered police, firefighters, and other first responders as everyday heroes—but not as superhumans. Even with this shift, some foundational hallmarks will endure. Let us explore some of those ideas now.

Technology

Characteristically, Adaptables are logged in, linked up, and the most technologically driven generation to live on earth.[5] As early media scholar Marshall McLuhan suggests, technology is an extension of our being, and nothing is more apparent as generations age and emerge. Mark McCrindle asserts that this generation's members "don't think about these technologies as tools. . . . They integrate them singularly into their lives."[6] For example, Adaptables use AI and virtual reality (VR) to engage in worlds they could not experience otherwise, from raising Hatchimals to climbing Machu Picchu in their own homes.[7]

AI and VR will continue to enhance experiences—but not fully replace them. For example, while Adaptables may not want to physically study abroad or travel to faraway lands in person, they do want to have unique experiences—and their VR goggles can take them to places they only dreamed of visiting. If they do travel, then they may want to experience smaller, less technological, or even more rural areas, where population density and the spread of viruses is limited. This generation might even engage in more personalized vacations, whereby they visit a physical place and work on a social or environmental issue, such as climate change, clean water, housing, and more for those less fortunate.[8]

Multiple Identities

Similar to Gen-Z and their millennial parents, this generation will have multiple identities.[9] Their online and real-world identities, however, will not be as distinct. The limited amount of time they spend with others will help them see the importance of identity continuity, somewhat diminishing the line between online and real-world selves. They will learn to express themselves with more authenticity so others can experience their identities no matter where they are—in essence, a secret identity may be a thing of the past.

Also, as we discussed in early chapters, Gen-Zers have second jobs, especially when it comes to social media branding and having paid side gigs, and the Adaptables and future generations will also have to create and sustain multiple identities. But these entrepreneurs will seek more ways to earn a living via social media (e.g., YouTube, Instagram, TikTok, whatever new platforms emerge) at much younger ages. They will use their fears and knowledge of unemployment and the Great Depression–like experiences to pave their own financial paths and do so early on.

Fear and Anxiety

In the same way that millennials and Gen-Zers deal with fear and anxiety, Adaptables will also contend with these emotions. Because of the constant, pervasive nature of negative news throughout the world, it is quite likely to exacerbate feelings of apprehension and worry. The influence from parents and caretakers could create feelings of foreboding and uneasiness in the lives of the next generation. While this will not be universally true, one can't help believing there will be an increase in anxiety and fear related to their realities. Couple these fears with being isolated, and there could be an even greater sense of angst than what was felt by Gen-Zers and millennials.

Economy

More economic inequality will also be the norm for Adaptables, as the gap between the rich and poor is exacerbated and the financial disparities between these groups grow. In early 2020, a record high unemployment rate in the United States is forecasted to lead to food shortages and financial despair, rivaling that of the Great Depression of 1929. What was once the norm for many children and adults will be changed, and opportunities for advancement on many levels are expected to dwindle.

Many Adaptables, like the silent generation one hundred years ago, will remember waiting in long lines or going through drive-through food pickups at local establishments to get their essentials. They will also remember their parents being furloughed or let go from their jobs due to the COVID-19 pandemic and the subsequent struggles that those experiences entail. Members of this generation will also likely remember that a trip to the store or eating in a restaurant requires more forethought, savings, and safety precautions. These early life experiences and world events will make them more financially and interpersonally cautious and require more activism in the face of adversity.

Education

Scott Galloway, a professor at New York University, predicted that the "post-pandemic future will entail [educational] partnerships between the largest tech companies in the world and elite universities."[10] He says he can envision MIT@Google, iStanford, or HarvardxFacebook. He believes this shift will allow for more people than ever to have access to a sound education, albeit offered through such tools as Google Hangouts and Zoom. While brick-and-mortar schools will not disappear altogether, those individuals who do have the opportunity to attend classes in person may very well come from the 1 percent.

While we will not know for a few years if Galloway's predictions come to fruition, we can predict that the Adaptables may prefer an in-person educational experience rather than one conducted remotely using technology. Early Gen-Alpha research suggests a preference exists for virtual or visual learning opportunities, but screen fatigue may change this generation's learning and professional-development preferences at home, in the classroom, and in the workplace. They may now crave science and math in-person, not in virtual or online settings. We anticipate an increased need for hands-on learning that involves real-world problem solving and critical thinking, which will be necessary, not optional. A move from virtual experiences to lived experiences will guide their learning and prepare them for the future, but this epiphany about the role of technology in their lives will only do so much.

Early claims about the Adaptables also suggest that this generation would be the most formally educated generation of all time, but this may not be true postpandemic.[11] When schools at all levels were suddenly moved online in the spring of 2020, the pitfalls of inequality, from paychecks and Internet access to health care and safe homes, became painfully obvious for many. Public and private schools, including colleges and universities, experienced unprecedented online and virtual classroom interactions that many believe were unequal to previous in-person educational experiences. K–12 students went from traditional learning experiences, whereby the teacher taught the material in school, to a student-led and parent-guided system of education, with little, if any, actual teaching from educators. It was plain to see that the educational system, at least in the United States, was not prepared to handle this level of online learning. What is more, when students do return to the classroom, their experiences will be far different. Many will remember that their teachers and other classmates had to wear face masks and take safety precautions, such as disinfecting their classrooms several times a day, sitting six feet away from classmates, and even restricted play during recess and lunch.

As of the writing of this book, the future of higher education is in danger, and the loss of revenue these institutions have experienced has led to closures, furloughs, mergers, reductions, and changed pedagogy. The changed pedagogy, specifically, has raised concern about the quality of education provided to students during the global pandemic, as well as revealed more important questions about the cost of a formal education moving forward. In fact, gap years may become quite common for high school seniors, and free or less expensive coursework and certifications may be the new go-to in lieu of expensive college educations. The Adaptables will still seek intellectual and skilled opportunities, thereby increasing their entrepreneurial spirit beyond that of Gen-Z, but they will do so in new ways and at far less cost than ever before.

Workplace

One could argue that the COVID-19 global pandemic proved to be the greatest catalyst for change in the workplace that we have seen since Henry Ford's assembly line. Josie Cox observes, "Remote working as a result of COVID-19 may have forced those naturally nervous about adopting new technologies to take the plunge—even embrace them—but in other cases it might have broadened a real or perceived rift between those identifying as digital natives and those not."[12]

Both employees and employers have had to shift their thinking and adapt to new work environments. Large companies, such as Twitter, announced that they would allow employees to work from home forever. Jennifer Christie, head of human resources for Twitter, said the company would "never probably be the same in the structure of its work. People who were reticent to work remotely will find that they really thrive that way. Managers who did not think they could manage teams that were remote will have a different perspective. I do think we won't go back."[13]

For the companies that do not adopt such policies, well, Adaptables will challenge the process going forward. No longer will it be acceptable for more senior employees to resist change. The Adaptables will search for opportunities and look outward for innovative solutions. They may be more open to experimenting, taking risks, and generating small wins, which will propel them to learn more and do more.

Diversity and Inclusion

As mentioned previously, the Gen-Z cohort consists of a diverse population, where Caucasians are the minority racial group in the United States, with those numbers anticipated to steadily decrease over time. The diversity that the Adaptables experience will be far different; they will identify and define themselves as multiracial, multiethnic, and political and religious nones and embrace more diversity of sexual identity than ever.[14] More families will consist of trans parents, gay and lesbian couples, and biracial and multiracial people, raising their children to be more accepting.

In the coming years, many new cultural labels will also emerge. This should lead to more acceptance of diversity, but it is a wait-and-see scenario, as the current political divisiveness in the United States seems to have led to more prominence of hate groups, speech, and crimes. The protests that raged throughout American cities, where thousands of people gathered to grieve and demand justice for George Floyd, a black man who died in police custody, and others, illustrates that diversity and equality will remain a vital cause.

CONCLUSION

Generations need each other in order to develop their own identities and make their marks in society. World events and experiences, both positive and negative, will continue to inform and shape generational personas. As with all previous generations, time will be the real sorcerer. For now, the Adaptables, while similar in some ways to their millennial parents and the Gen-Z cohort, will find their own way—eventually.

EPILOGUE

COVID-19 and the
US Presidential Election:
The Inevitable Impact on Gen-Z

As we came to the end of researching and writing this book, the historic COVID-19 pandemic spread across the globe quickly, severely, and without prejudice, forever changing millions of lives. At the same time, a politically divisive presidential election plagued America for months.

We cannot deny that these events will affect Gen-Z at a crucial time in their lives, just as they are reaching key milestones. We know that our upbringing, education, and the early years of our careers create a foundation upon which a great deal of our future is built. Much of their worldview now will be shaped by these events.

To that end, we offer some areas we believe will be influenced most:

- **Education:** Gen-Zers have been touted as smart, perhaps even smarter than their predecessors, the millennials. When COVID-19 hit, schools were shut down. Students were sent home. Parents and caregivers became teachers, and the inequity in online education soon reared its ugly head; the digital divide was now more recognizable as a socioeconomic status divide, too. The educational ramifications of this change have yet to be realized. In fact, we won't know the results for many years to come.

- **Employment:** Prior to the pandemic, older Gen-Zers were graduating into a strong economy. Now, many have been laid off or furloughed or have seen their roles eliminated altogether. College students saw internships evaporate and job offers vanish. Gen-Zers were supposed to have a different, more positive experience than their millennial predecessors. This is simply not the case any longer.

- **Political Wounds:** As election night in the United States moved toward election week, with President Joe Biden and Vice President Kamala Harris achieving victory, the American public saw former president Trump become unhinged. In the early-morning hours following the election, Trump began to claim voter fraud, inciting protests outside election halls where the ballots were being counted. Taking to Twitter, he fueled the flames of injustice, again uniting his base with false claims—a hallmark of his presidency. On the evening of November 5, 2020, the *New York Times* reported that the three major broadcast networks—ABC, CBS, and NBC—cut away from the president as he lobbed false claims about the integrity of the election during his press conference held at the White House.[1] MSNBC was the first outlet to break away from the president's news conference, after a mere thirty-five seconds. The others followed almost instantly. In chapter 5, we assert that Gen-Z would help preserve democracy and civil discourse. Early reports coming out of the Center for Information and Research on Civic Learning and Engagement (CIRCLE) at Tufts University claim that voters under age thirty preferred Biden and Harris, with young people of color voting for him by the largest margins. Kei Kawashima-Ginsberg, CIRCLE's director, noted that racism and climate change were among the top issues cited by young voters.[2] These findings are aligned with our research on Gen-Zers.

- **Fear and Anxiety:** Already a cohort dealing with anxiety, fear, depression, and other mental health challenges, Gen-Zers are now trying to cope with multiple changes that are proving too difficult to maneuver around. Their levels of anxiety may only increase as the pandemic rages on and as political tensions rise in America.

There is, however, hope:

- **Principled Superheroes Fighting for Just Causes:** The protests and riots after the deaths of George Floyd, Breonna Taylor, and more Black Americans illustrate to us that the passion Gen-Z feels is vibrant. The 2020 presidential election, the anniversary of the Nineteenth Amendment, and renewed interest in reaching equality between men and women, as well as Black, Indigenous, and People of Color (BIPOC), show us that this generation is ready to stand up for what they believe in. Movements are taking form through collective action and true change. This generation has been raised to take a stand, be heard, create change, and make a difference. This will stay consistent and grow.
- **Finance:** Studies have shown that Gen-Z is increasingly careful in making financial decisions. Watching their parents struggle with reduced hours, unemployment, or job loss is creating a generation of more fiscally responsible individuals.
- **Boundary Setting:** An unintended consequence of the pandemic showed us that many companies will continue to allow large numbers of their employees to work from home. The rise of such technologies as Zoom, Slack, and Google Hangouts connected people and illustrated how we could conduct business as usual no matter where we were. With these changes comes the need to set boundaries. Some individuals felt that as the pandemic continued, they were "living at work" rather than "working from home." Gen-Z will reinvigorate the work-life balance established by Gen-Xers.

We also believe the generation after Gen-Z, Generation Alpha—The Adaptables—will have little memory of the pandemic or the 2020 presidential election, but they will experience it through shared memories of family and friends, learn about it in school, and be influenced through how they live and work. What we know for certain is that the US presidential election and COVID-19 will leave an indelible mark on Gen-Z, the superhero generation, and Gen-Alpha, the Adaptables.

Our book centers on the innate power of the superhero. It seems to us that what the world needs more than ever is the resilience, agility, and courage of our Superhero Generation: Gen-Z.

NOTES

PREFACE

1. Dan Western, "The Top 22 Motivational Superhero Quotes," *WealthyGorilla*, accessed February 26, 2020, https://wealthygorilla.com/top-22-motivational-superhero-quotes/.

CHAPTER 1

1. Frank Giancola, "The Generation Gap: More Myth than Reality," *Human Resource Planning* 29, no. 4 (2006): 32.

2. "Persona," Oxford Learner's Dictionaries, accessed March 9, 2020, https://www.oxfordlearnersdictionaries.com/us/definition/english/persona?q=persona.

3. Neil Howe and William Strauss, *Millennials Rising: The Next Great Generation* (New York: Vintage Books, 2000), 45.

4. Ana Nunes de Almeida, Ana Delicado, Nuno de Almeida Alves, and Tiago Carvalho, "Internet, Children and Space: Revisiting Generational Attributes and Boundaries," *New Media and Society* 17, no. 9 (2015): 1436–53.

5. William H. Frey, "The US Will Become 'Minority White' in 2045, Census Projects," Brookings, September 10, 2018, https://www.brookings.edu/blog/the-avenue/2018/03/14/the-us-will-become-minority-white-in-2045-census-projects/.

6. Regina Luttrell and Natalia Flores, "Why Diversity and Inclusion Warrant PR's Rapt Attention," *PR Daily*, October 3, 2019, https://www.prdaily.com/why-diversity-and-inclusion-warrant-prs-rapt-attention/.

7. Howe and Strauss, *Millennials Rising*, 45; Betty R. Kupperschmidt, "Multi-generation Employees: Strategies for Effective Management," *Health Care Manager* 19, no. 1 (2000): 65–76, accessed April 10, 2020, https://europepmc.org/article/med/11183655; Regina Luttrell and Karen McGrath, *The Millennial Mindset: Unraveling Fact from Fiction* (Lanham, MD: Rowman & Littlefield, 2015); "USA QuickFacts," US Census Bureau, July 8, 2014, accessed August 14, 2014, https://www.census.gov/quickfacts/fact/table/US/PST045219.

8. Howe and Strauss, *Millennials Rising*.

9. Robert G. DelCampo, Lauren A. Haggerty, Meredith Jane Haney, and Lauren Ashley Knippel, *Managing the Multi-generational Workforce from the GI Generation to the Millennials* (Farnham, VT: Gower, 2010).

10. Thom S. Rainer and Jess W. Rainer, *The Millennials: Connecting to America's Largest Generation* (Nashville: B&H, 2011).

11. Editors of Time-Life Books, *Events That Shaped the Century* (Alexandria, VA: Time-Life Books, 1998).

12. Douglas O. Linder, "*State v. John Scopes* ('The Monkey Trial')," July 10, 2000, accessed August 31, 2014, http://law2.umkc.edu/faculty/projects/ftrials/scopes/evolut.htm.

13. "19th Amendment to the U.S. Constitution: Women's Right to Vote," National Archives and Records Administration, accessed August 31, 2014, https://www.archives.gov/historical-docs/19th-amendment.

14. Ben Wattenberg, "Stock Market Crash," PBS: The First Measured Century, accessed August 31, 2014, https://www.pbs.org/fmc/timeline/estockmktcrash.htm.

15. "Rosie the Riveter," History, accessed August 31, 2014, http://www.history.com/topics/world-war-ii/rosie-the-riveter.

16. "A Brief History of the Tuskegee Airmen," Red Tail Squadron, accessed August 31, 2014, http://www.redtail.org/the-airmen-a-brief-history/.

17. Nancy Bell and Marvin Narz, "Meeting the Challenges of Age Diversity in the Workplace," *CPA Journal* 77, no. 2 (2007), http://www.cpajournal.com/.

18. Sheryl Lindsell-Roberts, "Bridging the Multigenerational Divide," in *New Rules for Today's Workplace* (Boston: Houghton Mifflin Harcourt, 2011).

19. "Coronavirus Live Updates: New Restrictions on International Travel Brings Chaos to Many Airports," *New York Times*, March 15, 2020, www.nytimes.com/2020/03/15/world/coronavirus-live.html.

20. "Traditionalists, Baby Boomers, Generation X, Generation Y (and Generation Z) Working Together," United Nations Joint Staff Pension Fund, accessed

April 10, 2020, http://aspringer.weebly.com/uploads/1/3/6/4/1364481/designing _recruitment_selection___talent_management_model_tailored_to_meet_unjspfs_ business_development_nee.pdf.

21. Brent Green, *Marketing to Leading-Edge Baby Boomers* (Lincoln, NE: Writers Advantage, 2003).

22. Editors of Time-Life Books, *Events*; "America's Historical Documents."

23. "Boomers Envision Retirement 2011," AARP, June 1, 2011, accessed August 14, 2014, https://www.aarp.org/work/retirement-planning/info-06-2011/boomers-envision-retirement-2011.html.

24. Mary F. Henson, *Trends in the Income of Families and Persons in the United States, 1947–1964* (Washington, DC: US Department of Commerce, Bureau of the Census, 1967).

25. "History—*Brown v. Board of Education* Reenactment," United States Courts, accessed August 31, 2014, http://www.uscourts.gov/educational-resources/get-involved/federal-court-activities/brown-board-education-re-enactment/history.aspx.

26. John Lukacs, *A Short History of the Twentieth Century* (Cambridge, MA: Belknap Press, 2013), 171.

27. "The Silent Spring," Natural Resources Defense Council, accessed August 28, 2014, http://www.nrdc.org/health/pesticides/hcarson.asp.

28. Paul Taylor and George Gao, "Generation X: America's Neglected 'Middle Child,'" Pew Research Center, June 5, 2014, accessed August 15, 2014 https://www.pewresearch.org/fact-tank/2014/06/05/generation-x-americas-neglected-middle-child/.

29. Ann Hulbert, "Look Who's Parenting," *New York Times*, July 4, 2004, http://www.nytimes.com/2004/07/04/magazine/04WWLN.html.

30. Susan Gregory Thomas, "A Teacher's Guide to Generation X Parents," *Edutopia*, January 19, 2010, accessed August 15, 2014, https://www.edutopia.org/generation-x-parents-relationships-guide.

31. Jeff Gordinier, *X Saves the World: How Generation X Got the Shaft but Can Still Keep Everything from Sucking* (New York: Viking, 2008).

32. "Multigenerational Characteristics," Bruce Mayhew Consulting, accessed August 15, 2014, http://www.brucemayhewconsulting.com/index.cfm?id=20209.

33. "Backgrounder on the Three Mile Island Accident," US NRC, accessed September 1, 2014, http://www.nrc.gov/reading-rm/doc-collections/fact-sheets/3mile-isle.html.

34. "Miranda Rights," MirandaRights.org, accessed September 1, 2014, http://www.mirandarights.org/; "Thurgood Marshall Biography," Biography, accessed September 1, 2014, http://www.biography.com/people/thurgood-marshall-9400241.

35. "*Roe v. Wade* and Its Impact," US History, accessed September 1, 2014. http://www.ushistory.org/us/57d.asp.

36. "The Law," US Equal Employment Opportunity Commission, accessed September 1, 2014, http://www.eeoc.gov/eeoc/history/35th/thelaw/.

37. *After Stonewall*, directed by John Scagliotti, narrated by Melissa Etheridge (New York: First Run Features, 2005), DVD.

38. MilkFoundation.org, accessed September 1, 2014, http://milkfoundation.org/.

39. "Databases, Tables and Calculators by Subject," Bureau of Labor Statistics, accessed September 1, 2014, http://data.bls.gov/pdq/SurveyOutputServlet.

40. Brian Dunbar, "July 20, 1969: One Giant Leap for Mankind," NASA, accessed September 1, 2014, https://www.nasa.gov/mission_pages/apollo/apollo11.html.

41. "The Apple II," Computer History Museum, accessed September 1, 2014, http://www.computerhistory.org/revolution/personal-computers/17/300.

42. Jim McPherson, "Media History Timeline," 2002, accessed September 1, 2014, http://www.webpages.uidaho.edu/jamm445hart/timeline.htm.

43. DelCampo et al., *Managing the Multi-generational Workforce*; Lindsey Gerdes, *The Best Places to Launch a Career: Top Employers for Interns and New College Grads* (New York: McGraw-Hill, 2008).

44. Luttrell and McGrath, *Millennial Mindset*.

45. Chuck Underwood, *Generational Imperative: Understanding Generational Differences in the Workplace, Marketplace, and Living Room* (Miamisburg, OH: Generational Imperative, 2007).

46. Carol Elam, Terry Stratton, and Denise D. Gibson, "Welcoming a New Generation to College: The Millennial Students," *Journal of College Admission* 195 (2007): 20–25.

47. Luttrell and McGrath, *Millennial Mindset*.

48. Eddy S. W. Ng, Linda Schweitzer, and Sean T. Lyons, "New Generation, Great Expectations: A Field Study of the Millennial Generation," *Journal of Business and Psychology* 25, no. 2 (2010): 281–92.

49. Ron Zemke, Claire Raines, and Bob Filipczak, *Generations at Work: Managing the Clash of Boomers, Gen Xers, and Gen Yers in the Workplace*, 2nd ed. (New York: AMACOM, American Management Association, 2013).

50. Paul Taylor and Scott Keeter, eds., *Millennials: Confident. Connected. Open to Change* (Washington, DC: Pew Research Center, February 2010), http://www.pewsocialtrends.org/files/2010/10/millennials-confident-connected-open-to-change.pdf.

51. Jean M. Twenge, *Generation Me*, rev. ed. (New York: Apria Books, 2014).

52. Don Tapscott, *Grown Up Digital: How the Net Generation Is Changing Your World* (New York: McGraw-Hill, 2009).

53. Robert DeBard, "Millennials Coming to College," *New Directions for Student Services* 2004, no. 106 (2004): 33–45, https://doi.org/10.1002/ss.123.

54. Wesley Whistle, "A Look at Millennial Student Debt," *Forbes*, October 4, 2019, https://www.forbes.com/sites/wesleywhistle/2019/10/03/a-look-at-millennial -student-debt/#67a212a2437e.

55. Zemke, Raines, and Filipczak, *Generations at Work*.

56. Gerdes, *Best Places*.

57. Gerdes, *Best Places*.

58. Maureen Stout, *The Feel-Good Curriculum: The Dumbing Down of America's Kids in the Name of Self-Esteem* (Boston: Da Capo Press, 2007).

59. Stout, *Feel-Good Curriculum*.

60. Regina Luttrell, "Social Networking Sites in the Public Relations Classroom: A Mixed Methods Analysis of Undergraduate Learning Outcomes Using WordPress, Facebook, and Twitter," PhD diss., California Institute of Integral Studies, 2012.

61. Michael Winograd, "It's Official: Millennials Realigned American Politics in 2008," *Huffington Post*, November 17, 2008, accessed September 5, 2014, https://www.huffpost.com/entry/its-official-millennials_b_144357?guccounter=1 &guce_referrer=aHR0cHM6Ly93d3cuZ29vZ2xlLmNvbS88&guce_referrer_sig= AQAAADnGxfTSVlZJhWiJm2I5jBpHkDCdrMlxJZt-Gk7uOm0HspM6apiPPt LyR-THFkE2II8Xpz8xHlyQ98S98Ku1hrAQ0Rkr9IWPIei2BIBAcIaEvSt5Pq GHM7B-EhS5JLKohvjgs2ldAOp2Q7_Z4TXGNGUmcsF0cnEcu0LP0VHi5wHf.

62. Neil Howe, "Don't Worry, America: Millennials Still Want to Marry," *Forbes*, March 25, 2014, accessed September 29, 2014 https://www.forbes.com/ sites/realspin/2014/03/25/dont-worry-america-millennials-still-want-to-marry/ ?sh=612b957a4035.

CHAPTER 2

1. Lauren M. Shearer, "Marvel and DC Superhero Movies since 2000," IMDB, last modified September 26, 2012, accessed February 19, 2020, https://www.imdb. com/list/ls008923275/.

2. Travis Clark, "Every Confirmed DC Comics Movie Coming to Theaters, Including a Batman Reboot and 'Aquaman' Sequel," *Business Insider*, December 12, 2019, accessed February 19, 2020, https://www.businessinsider.com/every -confirmed-dc-comics-movie-details-release-dates-2019-12; Hilary Weaver, "Here Is Every Superhero Movie Coming Out for the Foreseeable Future,"

Esquire, October 23, 2019, accessed February 19, 2020, https://www.esquire.com/entertainment/movies/a29551205/upcoming-new-superhero-movies/.

3. Richard Edwards and Bradley Russell, "All the New Marvel TV Shows Coming in 2020 and Beyond," Games Radar, February 3, 2020, accessed February 19, 2020, https://www.gamesradar.com/new-marvel-tv-shows/; Rob Leane, "8 Superhero Games in Development or Rumored," Den of Geek, January 10, 2020, accessed February 19, 2020, https://www.denofgeek.com/us/games/278501/up coming-superhero-games; Nicholas Raymond, "Every Upcoming DC TV Show," Screen Rant, October 31, 2019, accessed February 19, 2020, https://screenrant.com/dc-tv-shows-upcoming/.

4. Luke Mastin, "Introduction," Basics of Philosophy, accessed January 16, 2020, https://www.philosophybasics.com/branch_ethics.html. The greater-good utilitarian philosophy referred to here is the one espoused by philosophers Jeremy Bentham and John Stuart Mill.

5. Graeme McMilan, "S.H.I.E.L.D. 101: Everything You Need to Know about Marvel's Spy Agency," *Wired*, September 24, 2013, accessed February 19, 2020, https://www.wired.com/2013/09/s-h-i-e-l-d-101-faq/.

CHAPTER 3

1. "Digiverse," Ninjago Wiki, accessed January 29, 2020, https://ninjago.fandom.com/wiki/Digiverse.

2. Michael Dimock, "Defining Generations: Where Millennials End and Generation Z Begins," Pew Research Center, January 17, 2019, accessed April 22, 2019, https://www.pewresearchcenter.org/fact-tank/2019/01/17/where-millennials-end-and-generation-z-begins/.

3. Denise Villa, Jason Dorsey, and Elli Denison, *The State of Gen Z 2018* (Austin, TX: Center for Generational Kinetics, Fall 2018), accessed February 24, 2020, https://genhq.com/wp-content/uploads/2018/10/State-of-Gen-Z-2018.pdf.

4. Katy Steinmetz, "Move Over, Millennials: How Generation Z Is Disrupting Work as We Know It," *Time*, December 15, 2017, https://time.com/5066641/generation-z-disruption/.

5. Jeff Schultz, "How Much Data Is Created on the Internet Each Day?" *Micro Focus* (blog), June 8, 2019, accessed February 24, 2020, https://blog.microfocus.com/how-much-data-is-created-on-the-internet-each-day/.

6. Sharon Florentine, "Everything You Need to Know about Generation Z," CIO, June 20, 2018, accessed April 19, 2019, https://www.cio.com/article/3282415/everything-you-need-to-know-about-generation-z.html.

7. Charlotte Alter, "The School Shooting Generation Has Had Enough," *Time*, March 22, 2018, 1–10, accessed January 18, 2020, https://time.com/longform/never-again-movement/.

8. David S. Meyer, "One Year after the Parkland Shooting, Is the #Never-Again Movement on Track to Succeed?" February 14, 2019, *Washington Post*, accessed January 18, 2020, http://thewashingtonpost.com/news/monkey-cage/wp/2019/02/14/one-year-after-the-parkland-shooting-is-the-neveragain-movement-on-track-to-succeed/.

9. Brianna Holt, "Gen-Zers on Tinder Want Someone to March With, Not Just Match With," Quartz, December 17, 2019, accessed February 3, 2020, https://qz.com/1769311/gen-z-is-putting-social-justice-issues-on-tinder-profiles/.

10. Bennett Bennett, "Levis Steps Up on Social Issues with Three-Pronged Support for Gun Control," Drum, September 4, 2018, https://www.thedrum.com/news/2018/09/04/levis-steps-up-social-issues-with-three-pronged-support-gun-control.

11. Christian Allaire, "Yes, Those Viral Patagonia Tags Are Real," *Vogue*, September 16, 2020, accessed November 6, 2020, https://www.vogue.com/article/patagonia-vote-tags-political-statement.

12. Edward Felsenthal, "Greta Thunberg: *Time*'s Person of the Year 2019," *Time*, December 11, 2019, 48–49, 50–67, accessed February 25, 2020, https://time.com/magazine/us/5748137/december-23rd-2019-vol-194-no-27-u-s/.

13. Leah Asmelash, "Great Thunberg Isn't Alone. Meet Some Other Young Activists Who Are Leading the Environmentalist Fight," CNN World, September 29, 2019, accessed January 31, 2020, https://www.cnn.com/2019/09/28/world/youth-environment-activists-greta-thunberg-trnd/index.html.

14. Abby Ohlheiser, "The Woman behind 'Me Too' Knew the Power of the Phrase When She Created It—10 Years Ago," *Washington Post*, October 19, 2017, accessed February 25, 2020, https://www.washingtonpost.com/news/the-intersect/wp/2017/10/19/the-woman-behind-me-too-knew-the-power-of-the-phrase-when-she-created-it-10-years-ago/; Nadia Khomami, "#MeToo: How a Hashtag Became a Rallying Cry against Sexual Harassment," *Guardian*, October 20, 2017, accessed February 25, 2020, https://www.theguardian.com/world/2017/oct/20/women-worldwide-use-hashtag-metoo-against-sexual-harassment.

15. "Sexual Harassment and Assault Allegations List," Vox, updated January 9, 2019, accessed January 28, 2020, https://www.vox.com/a/sexual-harassment-assault-allegations-list.

16. "In the News," The Elevator Project, 2016, https://www.theelevatorproject.org/in-the-news; Karen Zraick, "22 States Considered Eliminating the 'Tampon

Tax' This Year. Here's What Happened," *New York Times*, July 12, 2019, accessed February 3, 2020, https://www.nytimes.com/2019/07/12/us/tampon-tax.html.

17. Abbey White, "Fans Praise Jennifer Lopez for Puerto Rican Pride, Pro-Immigration Statement during Super Bowl Halftime," *Hollywood Reporter*, February 2, 2020, accessed February 3, 2020, https://www.hollywoodreporter.com/news/super-bowl-halftime-jennifer-lopez-praised-subtle-immigration-statements-1275653.

18. Jacob Geanous, "Children Stage Mass-Walkout after Teachers Were Forced to Quit for Being Gay," *Metro*, February 19, 2020, accessed February 25, 2020, https://metro.co.uk/2020/02/19/students-walk-class-catholic-school-forced-gay-teachers-quit-12269247/; Donald Judd, "'I Want to Be Brave Like You': 9-Year-Old Asks Pete Buttigieg to Help Him Tell the World He's Gay," CNN, February 23, 2020, accessed February 25, 2020, https://www.cnn.com/2020/02/23/politics/pete-buttigieg-denver-rally-moment/index.html.

19. Aaron Earls, "Facts and Trends: 10 Traits of Generation Z," Lifeway, September 29, 2017, accessed April 19, 2019, https://factsandtrends.net/2017/09/29/10-traits-of-generation-z/.

20. Anne Kingston, "Get Ready for Generation Z," *Maclean's*, July 21, 2014, 42–45, https://www.macleans.ca/society/life/get-ready-for-generation-z/.

21. Kennedy O'Neal, "Super Kennedy—Piggybank (Official Music Video)," video, 2:01, January 1, 2020, accessed February 24, 2020, https://www.youtube.com/watch?v=—gO_spXX-Q.

22. Madeline Berg, "The Highest-Paid YouTube Stars of 2019: The Kids Are Killing It," *Forbes*, December 18, 2019, accessed February 24, 2020, https://www.forbes.com/sites/maddieberg/2019/12/18/the-highest-paid-youtube-stars-of-2019-the-kids-are-killing-it/#190c9f7338cd.

23. Aly Weisman, "Here's How TMZ Got the Name TMZ," *Business Insider*, July 31, 2014, accessed February 2, 2020, https://www.businessinsider.com/what-does-tmz-stand-for-2014-7.

24. Paul Fahri, "TMZ Was First—Again. Will Its Word Alone Ever Be Good Enough for Traditional Media?" *Washington Post*, April 22, 2016, accessed February 2, 2020, https://www.washingtonpost.com/lifestyle/style/tmz-was-first—again-will-their-word-alone-ever-be-good-enough-for-traditional-media/2016/04/22/822613ae-0805-11e6-bdcb-0133da18418d_story.html; Mark Tracy, "In Haste to Confirm Kobe Bryant News, News Media Stumbles," *New York Times*, January 27, 2020, accessed February 2, 2020, https://www.nytimes.com/2020/01/27/business/tmz-kobe.html.

25. Jack Drescher, "Out of DSM: Depathologizing Homosexuality," *Behavioral Sciences* 5, no. 4 (December 2015): 565–75, accessed February 25, 2020, https://www.ncbi.nlm.nih.gov/pmc/articles/PMC4695779/.

26. Nicola Davies, "Nomophobia: Modern-Day Pathology," Psychiatry Advisor, September 18, 2018, accessed February 4, 2020, https://www.psychiatryadvisor .com/home/topics/anxiety/nomophobia-the-modern-day-pathology/.

27. Kingston, "Get Ready."

28. Michelle Crouch, "Generation Zzzzzzzz," *Choices*, September 2017, accessed February 25, 2020, 10–15, https://choices.scholastic.com/issues/2017-18/090117/ generation-zzzzzzzz.html.

29. See Carol Gilligan, *In a Different Voice: Psychological Theory and Women's Development* (1982; repr., Cambridge, MA: Harvard University Press, 2016); John Gray, *Men Are from Mars, Women Are from Venus: The Classic Guide to Understanding the Opposite Sex* (1992; repr., New York: HarperCollins, 2012).

30. Quoted in "Emotional Intelligence in Leadership: Learning How to Be More Aware," MindTools, accessed February 24, 2020, https://www.mindtools.com/ pages/article/newLDR_45.htm.

31. Regina Luttrell and Karen McGrath, *The Millennial Mindset: Unraveling Fact from Fiction* (Lanham, MD: Rowman & Littlefield, 2015).

32. Ernest J. Zarra, *Helping Parents Understand the Minds and Hearts of Generation Z* (Lanham, MD: Rowman & Littlefield, 2017).

33. Commscope, "The Generation Z Study of Tech Intimates," *Business Wire*, October 16, 2017, 8–9, accessed February 25, 2020, https://www.businesswire .com/news/home/20171016005473/en/CommScope-Research-Gen-Tech-Intimates -Reveals-Always-On.

34. Jim Paterson, "Class of 2017: The Good, the Bad, and What's Next," *Journal of College Admission*, no. 234 (Winter 2017): 45–46, accessed February 25, 2020, https://files.eric.ed.gov/fulltext/EJ1142215.pdf.

CHAPTER 4

1. Janice Gassam Asare, "How Generation Z Will Impact Your Workplace," *Forbes*, December 16, 2018, accessed June 19, 2019, https://www.forbes.com/ sites/janicegassam/2018/12/26/how-the-newest-generation-generation-z-will-impact -your-workplace/#2197348d2aff6; Dan Marzullo, "How to Motivate Generation Z at Work," Workest, October 15, 2019, accessed March 23, 2020, https://www .zenefits.com/workest/how-to-motivate-generation-z-at-work/.

2. Jon Gutierrez, Luke Y. Thompson, and Andy Hughes, "The 6 Worst Jobs Wonder Woman Ever Had," Topless Robot, September 4, 2015, https://www .toplessrobot.com/2011/03/the_6_worst_jobs_wonder_woman_ever_had.php.

3. Friedrich Weltzien, "Masque-ulinities: Changing Dress as a Display of Masculinity in the Superhero Genre," *Fashion Theory* 9, no. 2 (2005): 229–50, https://doi.org/10.2752/136270405778051374.

4. Asare, "Generation Z."

5. Anthony Turner, "Generation Z: Technology and Social Interest," *Journal of Individual Psychology* 71, no. 2 (Summer 2015): 108, https://doi.org/10.1353/jip.2015.0021.

6. Hallie Crawford, "A Guide to Managing Multiple Generations in the Workplace," *US News and World Report*, May 1, 2018, accessed March 23, 2020, https://money.usnews.com/money/blogs/outside-voices-careers/articles/2018-05-01/a-guide-to-managing-multiple-generations-in-the-workplace.

7. Živa Veingerl Čič and Simona Šarotar Žižek, "Intergenerational Cooperation at the Workplace from the Management Perspective," *Gospodarstvo/Our Economy* 63, no. 3 (2017): 47–59, accessed March 23, 2020, https://www.researchgate.net/publication/320021515_Intergenerational_Cooperation_at_the_Workplace_from_the_Management_Perspective.

8. Corey Seemiller and Meghan Grace, *Generation Z: A Century in the Making* (New York: Routledge, 2019), 242.

9. Interestingly, Gen-Zers have harnessed their love of video games to pay for higher education: Many colleges and universities around the world now have a growing interest and investment in e-sports teams. So, Gen-Zers, go earn money while playing *and* getting your education.

10. David Stillman and Jonah Stillman, *Gen Z @ Work: How the Next Generation Is Transforming the Workplace* (New York: HarperCollins, 2017), 224–47.

11. World Economic Forum, annual meeting, Davos-Klosters, Switzerland, January 20–23, 2016, accessed October 27, 2020, https://newclimateeconomy.net/content/world-economic-forum-annual-meeting-2016.

12. Regina Luttrell and Karen McGrath, *The Millennial Mindset: Unraveling Fact from Fiction* (Lanham, MD: Rowman & Littlefield, 2015), chap. 20.

13. Peter G. Northouse, *Leadership: Theory and Practice*, 6th ed. (Thousand Oaks, CA: Sage, 2013), 5.

14. Daniel Goleman, "What Makes a Leader?" in *HBR's 10 Must Reads on Emotional Intelligence* (Boston: Harvard Business Review Press, 2015), 1–21.

15. Richard Dool and a Team of GenZ Co-Authors, *How Generation Z Wants to Be Led* (Independently published, 2019), 39–53; Charles Eaton, "Mentoring the Next Generation of Technologists," *Tech Directions*, October 2017, 29, accessed March 26, 2020, 29, http://www.omagdigital.com/publication/?i=441544&article_id=2894683&view=articleBrowser&ver=html5.

16. Kira B. Copperman, *Gen-Speak: Communication Strategies for the New Generational Mix at Work* (Independently published, 2018), 119–34.

CHAPTER 5

1. Greg Lukianoff and Jonathan Haidt, *Coddling of the American Mind: How Good Intentions and Bad Ideas Are Setting Up a Generation for Failure* (New York: Penguin Press, 2018).

2. Alexander Burns, Matt Flegenheimer, Jasmine C. Lee, Lisa Lerer, and Jonathan Martin, "Who's Running for President in 2020," *New York Times*, updated February 19, 2020, accessed February 21, 2020, https://www.nytimes.com/interactive/2019/us/politics/2020-presidential-candidates.html.

3. Moustafa Bayoumi, "Justin Trudeau's Brownface Scandal Is Bad. But Voting Him Out Isn't the Solution," *Guardian*, September 20, 2019, accessed February 18, 2020, https://www.theguardian.com/commentisfree/2019/sep/20/justin-trudeau-brownface-scandal.

4. Hannah Schrelacher Blair, "Why the GOP Should Pay Attention to Gen Z," Real Clear Politics, August 22, 2019, accessed February 18, 2020, https://www.realclearpolitics.com/articles/2019/08/22/why_the_gop_should_pay_attention_to_gen_z__141066.html.

5. Ethan Gilsdorf, "What Makes Superheroes So Super?" WBUR, March 25, 2016, https://www.wbur.org/artery/2016/03/25/what-makes-superheroes-so-super.

6. "Malala Yousafzai: Facts," The Nobel Prize, accessed February 14, 2020, https://www.nobelprize.org/prizes/peace/2014/yousafzai/facts/.

7. Jazz Jennings, "When I First Knew I Was Transgender," *Time*, May 31, 2016, accessed February 14, 2020, https://time.com/4350574/jazz-jennings-transgender/.

8. Umesh Bhagchadanhi, "Why Genderqueer and LGBTQ+ Fashion Icon Jaden Smith Is Fighting for the Right to Self-Expression for His Generation," *South China Morning Post*, January 31, 2020, accessed February 14, 2020, https://www.scmp.com/magazines/style/celebrity/article/3048330/why-genderqueer-and-lgbtq-fashion-icon-jaden-smith.

9. Miriam Berger, "2019 in Review: A Roller Coaster Ride for Women's Rights and Gender Equality around the World," *Washington Post*, December 26, 2019, accessed February 14, 2020, https://www.washingtonpost.com/world/2019/12/23/review-roller-coaster-ride-womens-rights-gender-equality-around-world/.

10. Scottie Andrew, "Guns Rights Activist Kaitlin Bennett Swarmed by Student Protesters during Surprise Ohio University Visit," CNN, February 18, 2020,

accessed February 21, 2020, https://www.cnn.com/2020/02/18/us/kaitlin-bennett
-ohio-university-protests-trnd/index.html.

11. Beah Jacobson and Natalia Tramontana, "Seven Young Leaders Making
Black History Today," America's Promise Alliance, February 8, 2018, accessed
February 14, 2020, https://www.americaspromise.org/news/seven-young-leaders
-making-black-history-today.

12. "As of March 26, 2019, bump stocks are illegal for almost all US civilians, but
multiple lawsuits are pending that challenge that rule." See "Rules and Regulations:
Bump Stocks," Bureau of Alcohol, Tobacco, Firearms, and Explosives, updated
February 21, 2019, accessed February 18, 2020, https://www.atf.gov/rules-and
-regulations/bump-stocks.

13. Andrew, "Guns Rights Activist."

14. Esteban Ortiz-Ospina and Diana Beltekian, "Why Do Women Live Longer
than Men?" Our World in Data, August 14, 2018, accessed February 20, 2020,
https://ourworldindata.org/why-do-women-live-longer-than-men.

15. Pam Fessler, "US Census Bureau Reports Poverty Rate Down, but Millions
Still Poor," NPR, September 10, 2019, accessed February 14, 2020, https://www
.npr.org/2019/09/10/759512938/u-s-census-bureau-reports-poverty-rate-down
-but-millions-still-poor.

16. Christina Troitino, "Why Taco Bell's Viral $100,000 Salary Test Isn't Ridic-
ulous," *Forbes*, January 10, 2020, accessed February 21, 2020, https://www.forbes
.com/sites/christinatroitino/2020/01/10/why-taco-bells-viral-100000-salary-test-isnt
-ridiculous/#e626e7831f08.

17. Marina Pitofsky, "Child Pays Off Lunch Debt for Over 120 Classmates with
Stand Selling Cider, Cocoa and Cookies," *Hill*, December 17, 2019, accessed February 20, 2020, https://thehill.com/blogs/blog-briefing-room/news/474950-5-year
-old-pays-off-lunch-debt-for-over-120-classmates-with.

18. Larry Elliot, "World's 26 Richest People Own as Much as Poorest 50%,
Says Oxfam," *Guardian*, modified January 21, 2020, accessed February 2020,
https://www.theguardian.com/business/2019/jan/21/world-26-richest-people-own
-as-much-as-poorest-50-per-cent-oxfam-report.

19. Abigail Hess, "Tuition at Public Colleges Has Increased in All 50 States over
the Past 10 Years—Here's How Your State Compares," CNBC, October 24, 2019,
accessed February 14, 2020, https://www.cnbc.com/2019/10/24/college-costs-have
-increased-in-all-50-states-over-the-past-10-years.html.

20. "2019 Was 2nd Hottest Year on Record for Earth Say NOAA, NASA,"
National Oceanic and Atmospheric Administration, January 15, 2020, accessed February 21, 2020, https://www.noaa.gov/news/2019-was-2nd-hottest-year-on-record

-for-earth-say-noaa-nasa, Jonathan Watts, "Antarctic Temperature Rises above 20C for First Time on Record," *Guardian*, February 13, 2020, accessed February 20, 2020, https://www.theguardian.com/world/2020/feb/13/antarctic-temperature-rises -above-20c-first-time-record.

21. "Pipeline Failures and Our Water Supplies," American Rivers, accessed February 20, 2020, https://www.americanrivers.org/threats-solutions/energy -development/pipeline-failures/.

22. Matthew Farmer, "New Models Reveal Full Extent of Deepwater Horizon Spill Damage," Off-Shore Technology, February 17, 2020, accessed February 18, 2020, https://www.offshore-technology.com/news/deepwater-horizon-oil-spread -satellite/; Alison Rose Levy, "The Deepwater Horizon Oil Spill Was a Cover -Up, Not a Cleanup," TruthDig, February 17, 2020, accessed February 18, 2020, https://www.truthdig.com/articles/the-deepwater-horizon-oil-spill-was-a-cover-up -not-a-cleanup/.

23. "College Press Freedom and Censorship," Student Press Law Center, accessed February 21, 2020, https://splc.org/college/.

24. Lynda Edwards, "Albany's Gen Z Protests Abortion Differently," *Albany Times Union*, updated January 18, 2019, accessed February 18, 2020, https:// www.timesunion.com/news/article/Albany-s-Gen-Z-protests-abortion-differently -13539514.php.

25. "'Pro-Choice' or 'Pro-Life,' 2018–2019 Demographic Tables," Gallup, accessed February 18, 2020, "https://news.gallup.com/poll/244709/pro-choice-pro -life-2018-demographic-tables.aspx.

26. Michael Wines, "What Is Gerrymandering? And Why Did the Supreme Court Rule on It?" *New York Times*, June 27, 2019, accessed February 21, 2020, https://www.nytimes.com/2019/06/27/us/what-is-gerrymandering.html.

27. "Voting Laws Roundup 2019," Brennan Center for Justice, July 10, 2019, accessed February, 21, 2020, https://www.brennancenter.org/our-work/research -reports/voting-laws-roundup-2019.

CHAPTER 6

1. "Popular Western Canon Books," Goodreads, accessed October 29, 2020, https://www.goodreads.com/shelf/show/western-canon.

2. History.com Editors. "*Brown v. Board of Education*," History, updated February 21, 2020, accessed February 21, 2020, https://www.history.com/topics/black -history/brown-v-board-of-education-of-topeka.

3. History.com Editors, "Civil Rights Movement Timeline," History, updated January 16, 2020, accessed February 12, 2020, https://www.history.com/topics/civil-rights-movement/civil-rights-movement-timeline.

4. Sarah Pruitt, "What Happened at the Stonewall Riots? A Timeline of the 1969 Uprising," History, updated June 28, 2019, accessed February 12, 2020, https://www.history.com/news/stonewall-riots-timeline; "Second-Wave Feminism," Khan Academy, accessed February 12, 2020, https://www.khanacademy.org/humanities/us-history/postwarera/1960s-america/a/second-wave-feminism.

5. See the "banking concept" discussed in Paulo Freire, *Pedagogy of the Oppressed*, 30th anniversary ed., trans. Myra Bergman Ramos (New York: Continuum, 2000).

6. Jerry M. Lewis and Thomas R. Hensley, "The May 4 Shootings at Kent State University: The Search for Historical Accuracy," Kent State University, accessed February 10, 2020, https://www.kent.edu/may-4-historical-accuracy.

7. As a measurement of how far technology in education has come, for one author, 1983 brought her senior year of high school—and her first experience with a computer.

8. E. D. Hirsch Jr., *Cultural Literacy: What Every American Needs to Know* (New York: Houghton-Mifflin, 1987).

9. Heather Watson, "How Obsessed Is Gen Z with Mobile Technology," Center for Generational Kinetics, accessed February 13, 2020, https://genhq.com/how-obsessed-is-gen-z-with-mobile-technology/.

10. Andrew M. I. Lee, "No Child Left Behind (NCLB): What You Need to Know," Understood, accessed February 10, 2020, https://www.understood.org/en/school-learning/your-childs-rights/basics-about-childs-rights/no-child-left-behind-nclb-what-you-need-to-know.

11. Shira Ackerman and Kelsey Kloss, "The Guide to 3rd Grade," Scholastic, July 3, 2019, accessed February 10, 2020, https://www.scholastic.com/parents/school-success/school-success-guides/guide-to-3rd-grade.html.

12. Matthew Lynch, "7 Examples of Project-Based Learning Activities," Tech Advocate, October 19, 2017, accessed February 26, 2020, https://www.thetechedvocate.org/7-examples-project-based-learning-activities/.

13. Gardner Institute, accessed February 11, 2020, https://www.jngi.org/; Vivek Pandit, *We Are Generation Z: How Identity, Attitudes, and Perspectives Are Shaping Our Future* (Dallas: Brown Books, 2015), 71–72.

14. Thomas J. Tobin and Kirsten T. Behling, *Reach Everyone, Teach Everyone: Universal Design for Learning in Higher Education* (Morgantown: University of West Virginia Press, 2018).

15. Tobin and Behling, *Reach Everyone*, 134.

16. Jean M. Twenge, *iGen: Why Today's Super-Connected Kids Are Growing Up Less Rebellious, More Tolerant, Less Happy—and Completely Unprepared for Adulthood: And What It Means for the Rest of Us* (New York: Atria Books, 2018), 97.

17. Greg Lukianoff and Jonathan Haidt, *The Coddling of the American Mind: How Good Intentions and Bad Ideas Are Setting Up a Generation for Failure* (New York: Penguin Press, 2018).

18. Andrew Katz, "Unrest in Virginia," *Time*, accessed February 11, 2020, https://time.com/charlottesville-white-nationalist-rally-clashes/.

19. Corey Seemiller and Meghan Grace, *Generation Z Goes to College* (San Francisco: Jossey-Bass, 2016), 179.

20. Pandit, *We Are Generation Z*, 73.

CHAPTER 8

1. In *The Millennial Mindset: Unraveling Fact from Fiction*, we refer to Generation Z as "NEOs" or "neomillennials" based on research at that time. In this book we refer to them as Gen-Z.

2. Regina Luttrell and Karen McGrath, *The Millennial Mindset: Unraveling Fact from Fiction* (Lanham, MD: Rowman & Littlefield, 2017).

3. Jay Donovan, "The Average Age for a Child Getting Their First Smartphone Is Now 10.3 Years," TechCrunch, May 19, 2016, accessed February 6, 2020, https://techcrunch.com/2016/05/19/the-average-age-for-a-child-getting-their-first-smartphone-is-now-10-3-years/.

4. "Contradistinction," Dictionary.com, accessed February 6, 2020, https://www.dictionary.com/browse/contradistinctive.

5. Jill Manoff, "5 Gen-Z Influencers You Need to Know," Digiday, June 6, 2019, accessed February 6, 2020, https://digiday.com/marketing/5-gen-z-influencers-know/.

6. Deenie Hartzog-Mislock and Seeta Kanhai, "Meet 6 Gen Z Activists That Are Setting an Extraordinary Example," Refinery29, April 1, 2019, accessed January 21, 2020, https://www.refinery29.com/en-us/gen-z-female-entrepreneurs.

7. Deep Patel, "10 Gen Z Experts You Should Be Following," *Forbes*, July 6, 2017, accessed January 21, 2020, https://www.forbes.com/sites/deeppatel/2017/07/06/10-gen-z-experts-you-should-be-following/#404fa68e69cc.

8. Lauren Lee, "California Teen Donates More than 150 Coronavirus Sanitation Kits to the Homeless. Now She Wants Your Help to Distribute More," CNN, March 19, 2020, https://www.cnn.com/2020/03/19/us/teen-donates-sanitization-kits-to-homeless-iyw-trnd/index.html.

9. Sophie Hirsh, "13-Year-Old Vegan Climate Activist Genesis Butler Is on a Mission to Make the World a Kinder Place," GreenMatters, accessed November 5, 2020, https://www.greenmatters.com/p/genesis-butler-vegan-climate-activist.

10. *Entrepreneur* Staff, "41 Percent of Gen Z-ers Plan to Become Entrepreneurs (Infographic)," *Entrepreneur*, January 15, 2019, accessed January 21, 2020, https://www.entrepreneur.com/article/326354.

11. Benjamin Hardy, "The Most Potent Gen-Z Entrepreneurial Panel Assembled," Inc.com, August 25, 2018, accessed January 21, 2020, https://www.inc.com/benjamin-p-hardy/the-most-potent-gen-z-entrepreneurial-panel-assembled.html.

12. Hardy, "Most Potent Gen-Z."

13. Maayan, "Queeng Playing Cards," Indiegogo, accessed January 28, 2020, https://www.indiegogo.com/projects/queeng-playing-cards#/.

14. Julian E. Lange, Abdul Ali, Candida G. Brush, Andrew C. Corbett, Donna J. Kelley, Phillip H. Kim, and Mahdi Majbouri, *2017 United States Report: Global Entrepreneurship Monitor: National Entrepreneurial Assessment for the United States of America* (Babson Park, MA: Babson College, 2018), accessed January 21, 2020, https://www.babson.edu/media/babson/site-assets/content-assets/academics/centers-and-institutes/the-arthur-m-blank-center-for-entrepreneurship/global-research/GEM_USA_2017.pdf.

15. "FLEX On-Demand Transit," Capital District Transportation Authority, accessed February 5, 2020, https://www.cdta.org/flex.

16. "9 of the Biggest Social Media Influencers on Instagram," Digital Marketing Institute, accessed January 21, 2020, https://digitalmarketinginstitute.com/en-us/blog/9-of-the-biggest-social-media-influencers-on-instagram.

17. Seth Flaxman, Sharad Goel, and Justin M. Rao, "Filter Bubbles, Echo Chambers, and Online News Consumption," in "Party Polarization," special issue, *Public Opinion Quarterly* 80, no. S1 (2016): 298–320.

18. Daniel Goleman and Richard E. Boyatzis, "Emotional Intelligence Has 12 Elements. Which Do You Need to Work On?" *Harvard Business Review*, February 6, 2017, bit.ly/HRBEmotionalIntelligence; Jeanne Segal, Melinda Smith, Lawrence Robinson, and Jennifer Shubin, "Improving Emotional Intelligence (EQ)," HelpGuide, October 2019, bit.ly/HelpGuideEQ.

19. "Bullying Prevention," American Institutes for Research, September 28, 2020, bit.ly/AIRBullyingPrevention; StopBullying.gov, accessed November 1, 2020, https://www.stopbullying.gov/; Workplace Bullying Institute, accessed November 1, 2020, https://www.workplacebullying.org.

20. Alyssa Satara, "In 2 Sentences Elon Musk Explains Why the Key to Success Is Failure," Inc.com, April 30, 2018, retrieved February 6, 2020, https://www.inc

.com/alyssa-satara/in-2-sentences-elon-musk-explains-why-key-to-success-is-failure
.html.

21. See Jon Kabat-Zinn, "Guided Mindfulness Meditation Practices with Jon Kabat-Zinn," Mindfulnesscds.com, accessed November 1, 2020, https://www .mindfulnesscds.com/; Mindful, accessed November 1, 2020, https://www.mindful .org/; Kira M. Newman, "Free Mindfulness Apps Worthy of Your Attention," Mindful, November 18, 2019, accessed February 5, 2020, https://www.mindful.org/free -mindfulness-apps-worthy-of-your-attention/.

22. Kessler, Glenn, Salvador Rizzo, and Meg Kelly. "President Trump has made more than 20,000 false or misleading claims." *The Washington Post.* Last modified July 13, 2020. https://www.washingtonpost.com/politics/2020/07/13/president-trump-has-made-more-than-20000-false-or-misleading-claims/.

23. FactCheck.org, accessed November 1, 2020, https://www.factcheck.org/; Politifact, accessed November 1, 2020, https://www.politifact.com/.

24. See Thomas Cathcart, *The Trolley Problem: Or Would You Throw the Fat Guy Off the Bridge? A Philosophical Conundrum* (New York: Workman, 2013).

25. "Trolley Problem," Wikipedia, accessed March 29, 2020, https://en .wikipedia.org/wiki/Trolley_problem.

26. "Code of Ethics," National Education Association, September 14, 2020, https://www.nea.org/resource-library/code-ethics.

27. "Emotional Intelligence: What Teachers Can Do," Edutopia, February 22, 2001, https://www.edutopia.org/take-action-what-teachers-can-do.

28. "What Is Kahoot!?" Kahoot, accessed February 6, 2020, https://kahoot.com/ what-is-kahoot/.

29. "What Is Universal Design," Centre for Excellence in Universal Design, accessed March 31, 2020, http://universaldesign.ie/What-is-Universal-Design/.

30. ERIC Institute of Education Sciences, accessed November 1, 2020, https:// eric.ed.gov/.

31. Quoted in Barnaby Lashbrooke, "Want More from Generation Z? Mentor, Don't Manage Them," *Forbes*, June 24, 2019, https://www.forbes.com/sites/ barnabylashbrooke/2019/06/21/want-more-from-generation-z-mentor-dont-manage -them/#52f6ae505530.

CHAPTER 9

1. Caroline Bologna, "What Do We Call the Generation after Gen-Z?" Huff-Post, November 8, 2019, https://www.huffpost.com/entry/generation-alpha-after -gen-z_l_5d420ef4e4b0aca341181574.

2. Alex Williams, "Meet Alpha: The Next 'Next' Generation," *New York Times*, September 19, 2015, http://www.nytimes.com/2015/09/19/fashion/meet-alpha-the -next-next-generation.html.

3. Susan Fourtané, "Generation Alpha: The Children of the Millennial," Interesting Engineering, December 18, 2018, https://interestingengineering.com/ generation-alpha-the-children-of-the-millennial.

4. Adrienne Pasquarelli and E. J. Schultz, "Move Over Gen Z, Generation Alpha Is the One to Watch," *Ad Age*, January 22, 2019, https://adage.com/article/cmo -strategy/move-gen-z-generation-alpha-watch/316314.

5. "Gen Z and Gen Alpha Infographic Update," McCrindle, February 15, 2020, https://mccrindle.com.au/insights/blogarchive/gen-z-and-gen-alpha-infographic -update/.

6. Quoted in Christina Sterbenz, "Here's Who Comes after Generation Z—and They'll Be the Most Transformative Age Group Ever," *Business Insider*, December 5, 2015, accessed April 28, 2020, https://www.buinessinsider.com/generation-alpha -2014-7-2.

7. Victoria Turk, "Understanding Generation Alpha," *Wired*, October 17, 2017, accessed April 28, 2020, https://www.wired.co.uk/article/understanding -generation-alpha.

8. Who Is Generation Alpha and Are They Going to Change the Travel Industry?" Travel Technology and Solutions, May 10, 2019, accessed April 28, 2020, http://www.tts.com/blog/who-is-generation-alpha-and-are-they-going-to-change -the-travel-industry/.

9. Kimberly Zapata, "Meet Generation Alpha. Here's How Their Lives Will Be Different than Previous Generations," BestLife, August 13, 2019, https://bestlife online.com/generation-alpha-facts/.

10. James D. Walsh, "The Coming Disruption: Scott Galloway Predicts a Handful of Elite Cyborg Universities Will Soon Monopolize Higher Education," Intelligencer, May 11, 2020, https://nymag.com/intelligencer/2020/05/scott-galloway -future-of-college.html.

11. Ursula Perano, "Meet Generation Alpha, the 9-Year-Olds Shaping Our Future," Axios, August 8, 2019, https://www.axios.com/generation-alpha-millennial -children-63438b10-6817-483e-8472-38810df77880.html.

12. Josie Cox, "Gen Z, Millennials and Co: Why COVID-19 Makes It More Important than Ever for Companies to Understand the Multigenerational Workforce," *Forbes*, April 28, 2020, https://www.forbes.com/sites/josie cox/2020/04/28/genz-millennials-coronavirus-covid-19-boomers-multigenerational -challenge/#50a3046e7acc.

13. Alan Kantrowitz, "Twitter Will Allow Employees to Work at Home Forever," Buzzfeed, May 12, 2020, https://www.buzzfeednews.com/article/alexkantrowitz/twitter-will-allow-employees-to-work-at-home-forever.

14. Sarah Cottrell, "Who Is Generation Alpha?" *Parents*, January 2, 2020, http://www.parents.com/parenting/better-parenting/style/who-is-generation-alpha/.

EPILOGUE

1. Michael M. Grynbaum and Tiffany Hsu, "Major Networks Cut Away from Trump's Baseless Fraud Claims," *New York Times*, November 5, 2020, accessed November 6, 2020, https://www.nytimes.com/2020/11/05/business/media/trump-tv.html.

2. Elizabeth Redden, "Young Voters Preferred Biden—With 1 Exception," Inside Higher Ed, last modified November 5, 2020, accessed November 6, 2020, https://insidehighered.com/news/2020/11/05/analysis-sheds-first-light-youth-voting-trends.

BIBLIOGRAPHY

AARP. "Boomers Envision Retirement 2011." June 1, 2011. Accessed August 14, 2014. https://www.aarp.org/work/retirement-planning/info-06-2011/boomers -envision-retirement-2011.html.

Ackerman, Shira, and Kelsey Kloss. "The Guide to 3rd Grade." Scholastic. July 3, 2019. Accessed February 10, 2020. https://www.scholastic.com/parents/school -success/school-success-guides/guide-to-3rd-grade.html.

Allaire, Christian. "Yes, Those Viral Patagonia Tags Are Real." *Vogue*, September 16, 2020. Accessed November 6, 2020. https://www.vogue.com/article/patagonia -vote-tags-political-statement.

Alter, Charlotte. "The School Shooting Generation Has Had Enough." *Time*, March 22, 2018. Accessed January 18, 2020. https://time.com/longform/never -again-movement/.

American Institutes for Research. "Bullying Prevention." September 28, 2020. bit .ly/AIRBullyingPrevention.

American Rivers. "Pipeline Failures and Our Water Supplies." Accessed February 20, 2020. https://www.americanrivers.org/threats-solutions/energy-development/ pipeline-failures/.

Andrew, Scottie. "Guns Rights Activist Kaitlin Bennett Swarmed by Student Pro-testers during Surprise Ohio University Visit." CNN. February 18, 2020. Ac-cessed February 21, 2020. https://www.cnn.com/2020/02/18/us/kaitlin-bennett -ohio-university-protests-trnd/index.html.

Asare, Janice Gassam. "How Generation Z Will Impact Your Workplace." *Forbes*, December 26, 2018. Retrieved June 19, 2019. https://www.forbes.com/sites/ janicegassam/2018/12/26/how-the-newest-generation-generation-z-will-impact -your-workplace/#3afbb9692af6.

Asmelash, Leah. "Greta Thunberg Isn't Alone. Meet Some Other Young Activists Who Are Leading the Environmentalist Fight." CNN World. September 29, 2019. Accessed January 31, 2020. https://www.cnn.com/2019/09/28/world/ youth-environment-activists-greta-thunberg-trnd/index.html.

Bayoumi, Moustafa. "Justin Trudeau's Brownface Scandal Is Bad. But Voting Him Out Isn't the Solution." *Guardian*, September 20, 2019. Accessed February 18, 2020. https://www.theguardian.com/commentisfree/2019/sep/20/justin-trudeau -brownface-scandal.

Bell, Nancy, and Marvin Narz. "Meeting the Challenges of Age Diversity in the Workplace." *CPA Journal* 77, no. 2 (2007). http://www.cpajournal.com/.

Bennett, Bennett. "Levis Steps Up on Social Issues with Three-Pronged Support for Gun Control." Drum. September 4, 2018. https://www.thedrum.com/news/ 2018/09/04/levis-steps-up-social-issues-with-three-pronged-support-gun-control.

Berg, Madeline. "The Highest-Paid YouTube Stars of 2019: The Kids Are Killing It." *Forbes*, December 18, 2019. Accessed February 24, 2020. https:// www.forbes.com/sites/maddieberg/2019/12/18/the-highest-paid-youtube-stars -of-2019-the-kids-are-killing-it/#190c9f7338cd.

Berger, Miriam. "2019 in Review: A Roller Coaster Ride for Women's Rights and Gender Equality around the World." *Washington Post*, December 26, 2019. Accessed February 14, 2020. https://www.washingtonpost.com/world/2019/12/23/ review-roller-coaster-ride-womens-rights-gender-equality-around-world/.

Bhagchadanhi, Umesh. "Why Genderqueer and LGBTQ+ Fashion Icon Jaden Smith Is Fighting for the Right to Self-Expression for His Generation." *South China Morning Post*, January 31, 2020. Accessed February 14, 2020. https:// www.scmp.com/magazines/style/celebrity/article/3048330/why-genderqueer -and-lgbtq-fashion-icon-jaden-smith.

Biography. "Thurgood Marshall Biography." Accessed September 1, 2014. http:// www.biography.com/people/thurgood-marshall-9400241.

Blair, Hannah Schrelacher. "Why the GOP Should Pay Attention to Gen Z." Real Clear Politics. August 22, 2019. Accessed February 18, 2020. https://www .realclearpolitics.com/articles/2019/08/22/why_the_gop_should_pay_attention_ to_gen_z__141066.html.

Bologna, Caroline. "What Do We Call the Generation after Gen-Z?" HuffPost . November 8, 2019. Accessed May 5, 2020. https://www.huffpost.com/entry/ generation-alpha-after-gen-z_l_5d420ef4e4b0aca341181574.

Brennan Center for Justice. "Voting Laws Roundup 2019." July 10, 2019. Accessed February, 21, 2020. https://www.brennancenter.org/our-work/research-reports/voting-laws-roundup-2019.

Bruce Mayhew Consulting. "Multigenerational Characteristics." Accessed August 15, 2014. http://www.brucemayhewconsulting.com/index.cfm?id=20209.

Bureau of Alcohol, Tobacco, Firearms, and Explosives. "Rules and Regulations: Bump Stocks." Updated February 21, 2019. Accessed February 18, 2020. https://www.atf.gov/rules-and-regulations/bump-stocks.

Bureau of Labor Statistics. "Databases, Tables and Calculators by Subject." Accessed September 1, 2014. http://data.bls.gov/pdq/SurveyOutputServlet.

Burns, Alexander, Matt Flegenheimer, Jasmine C. Lee, Lisa Lerer, and Jonathan Martin. "Who's Running for President in 2020." *New York Times*, February 19, 2020. Accessed February 21, 2020. https://www.nytimes.com/interactive/2019/us/politics/2020-presidential-candidates.html.

Capital District Transportation Authority. "FLEX On-Demand Transit." Accessed February 5, 2020. https://www.cdta.org/flex.

Cathcart, Thomas. *The Trolley Problem: Or Would You Throw the Fat Guy Off the Bridge? A Philosophical Conundrum.* New York: Workman, 2013.

Centre for Excellence in Universal Design. "What Is Universal Design." Accessed March 31, 2020. http://universaldesign.ie/What-is-Universal-Design/.

Čič, Živa Veingerl, and Simona Šarotar Žižek. "Intergenerational Cooperation at the Workplace from the Management Perspective." *Gospodarstvo/Our Economy*, 63, no. 3 (2017): 47–59. https://doi.org/10.1515/ngoe-2017-0018.

Clark, Travis. "Every Confirmed DC Comics Movie Coming to Theaters, Including a Batman Reboot and 'Aquaman' Sequel." *Business Insider*, December 12, 2019. Accessed February 19, 2020. https://www.businessinsider.com/every-confirmed-dc-comics-movie-details-release-dates-2019-12.

Commscope. "The Generation Z Study of Tech Intimates." *Business Wire*, October 16, 2017. Accessed February 25, 2020. https://www.businesswire.com/news/home/20171016005473/en/CommScope-Research-Gen-Tech-Intimates-Reveals-Always-On.

Computer History Museum. "The Apple II." Accessed September 1, 2014. http://www.computerhistory.org/revolution/personal-computers/17/300.

Copperman, Kira B. 2018. *Gen-Speak: Communication Strategies for the New Generational Mix at Work.* Independently published.

"Coronavirus Live Updates: New Restrictions on International Travel Brings Chaos to Many Airports." *New York Times*, March 15, 2020. Updated March 25, 2020. https://www.nytimes.com/2020/03/15/world/coronavirus-live.html.

Cottrell, Sarah. "Who Is Generation Alpha?" *Parents*, January 2, 2020. Accessed April 30, 2020. https://www.parents.com/parenting/better-parenting/style/who-is-generation-alpha/.

Cox, Josie. "Gen Z, Millennials and Co: Why COVID-19 Makes It More Important than Ever for Companies to Understand the Multigenerational Workforce." *Forbes*, April 28, 2020. https://www.forbes.com/sites/josiecox/2020/04/28/genz-millennials-coronavirus-covid-19-boomers-multigenerational-challenge/#50a3046e7acc.

Crawford, Hallie. "A Guide to Managing Multiple Generations in the Workplace." *US News and World Report*, May 1, 2018. Accessed March 23, 2020. https://money.usnews.com/money/blogs/outside-voices-careers/articles/2018-05-01/a-guide-to-managing-multiple-generations-in-the-workplace.

Crouch, Michelle. "Generation Zzzzzzzz." *Choices*, September 2017. Accessed February 25, 2020. https://choices.scholastic.com/issues/2017-18/090117/generation-zzzzzzzz.html.

Davies, Nicola. "Nomophobia: Modern-Day Pathology." Psychiatry Advisor. September 18, 2018. Accessed February 4, 2020. https://www.psychiatryadvisor.com/home/topics/anxiety/nomophobia-the-modern-day-pathology/.

de Almeida, Ana Nunes, Ana Delicado, Nuno de Almeida Alves, and Tiago Carvalho. "Internet, Children and Space: Revisiting Generational Attributes and Boundaries." *New Media and Society* 17, no. 9 (2015): 1436–53.

DeBard, Robert. "Millennials Coming to College." *New Directions for Student Services* 106 (2004): 33–45. https://doi.org/10.1002/ss.123.

DelCampo, Robert G., Lauren A. Haggerty, Meredith Jane Haney, and Lauren Ashley Knippel. *Managing the Multi-generational Workforce from the GI Generation to the Millennials*. Farnham, VT: Gower, 2010.

Dictionary.com. "Contradistinction." Accessed February 6, 2020. https://www.dictionary.com/browse/contradistinctive.

Digital Marketing Institute. "9 of the Biggest Social Media Influencers on Instagram." Accessed January 21, 2020. https://digitalmarketinginstitute.com/en-us/blog/9-of-the-biggest-social-media-influencers-on-instagram.

Dimock, Michael. "Defining Generations: Where Millennials End and Generation Z Begins." Pew Research Center. January 17, 2019. Accessed April 22, 2019. https://www.pewresearch.org/fact-tank/2019/01/17/where-millennials-end-and-generation-z-begins/.

Donovan, Jay. "The Average Age for a Child Getting Their First Smartphone Is Now 10.3 Years." TechCrunch. May 19, 2016. Accessed February 6, 2020. https://techcrunch.com/2016/05/19/the-average-age-for-a-child-getting-their-first-smartphone-is-now-10-3-years/.

Dool, Richard, and a Team of Gen Z Co-Authors. *How Generation Z Wants to Be Led.* Independently published, 2019.

Drescher, Jack. "Out of DSM: Depathologizing Homosexuality." *Behavioral Sciences* 5, no. 4 (December 2015): 565–75. Accessed February 25, 2020. https://www.ncbi.nlm.nih.gov/pmc/articles/PMC4695779/.

Dunbar, Brian. "July 20, 1969: One Giant Leap for Mankind." NASA. Accessed September 1, 2014. https://www.nasa.gov/mission_pages/apollo/apollo11.html.

Earls, Aaron. "Facts and Trends: 10 Traits of Generation Z." Lifeway. September 29, 2017. Accessed April 19, 2019. https://factsandtrends.net/2017/09/29/10-traits-of-generation-z/.

Eaton, Charles. "Mentoring the Next Generation of Technologists." *Tech Directions*, October 2017. Accessed March 26, 2020. http://www.omagdigital.com/publication/?i=441544&article_id=2894683&view=articleBrowser&ver=html5.

Editors of Time-Life Books. *Events That Shaped the Century.* Alexandria, VA: Time-Life Books, 1998.

Edutopia. "Emotional Intelligence: What Teachers Can Do." February 22, 2001. https://www.edutopia.org/take-action-what-teachers-can-do.

Edwards, Lynda. "Albany's Gen Z Protests Abortion Differently." *Albany Times Union*, January 18, 2019. Accessed February 18, 2020. https://www.timesunion.com/news/article/Albany-s-Gen-Z-protests-abortion-differently-13539514.php.

Edwards, Richard, and Bradley Russell. "All the New Marvel TV Shows Coming in 2020 and Beyond." Games Radar. February 3, 2020. Accessed February 19, 2020. https://www.gamesradar.com/new-marvel-tv-shows/.

Elam, Carol, Terry Stratton, and Denise D. Gibson. "Welcoming a New Generation to College: The Millennial Students." *Journal of College Admission* 195 (2007): 20–25.

The Elevator Project. "In the News." 2016. https://www.theelevatorproject.org/in-the-news.

Elliot, Larry. "World's 26 Richest People Own as Much as Poorest 50%, Says Oxfam." *Guardian*, January 21, 2020. Accessed February 2020. https://www.theguardian.com/business/2019/jan/21/world-26-richest-people-own-as-much-as-poorest-50-per-cent-oxfam-report.

Entrepreneur Staff. "41 Percent of Gen Z-ers Plan to Become Entrepreneurs (Infographic)." *Entrepreneur*, January 15, 2019. Accessed January 21, 2020. https://www.entrepreneur.com/article/326354.

ERIC Institute of Education Sciences. Accessed November 1, 2020. https://eric.ed.gov/.

FactCheck.org. Accessed November 1, 2020. https://www.factcheck.org/.

Fahri, Paul. "TMZ Was First—Again. Will Its Word Alone Ever Be Good Enough for Traditional Media?" *Washington Post*, April 22, 2016. Accessed February 2, 2020.

https://www.washingtonpost.com/lifestyle/style/tmz-was-first—again-will-their
-word-alone-ever-be-good-enough-for-traditional-media/2016/04/22/822613ae
-0805-11e6-bdcb-0133da18418d_story.html.

Farmer, Matthew. "New Models Reveal Full Extent of Deepwater Horizon Spill
Damage." Off-Shore Technology. February 17, 2020. Accessed February 18,
2020. https://www.offshore-technology.com/news/deepwater-horizon-oil-spread
-satellite/.

Felsenthal, Edward. "Greta Thunberg: *Time*'s Person of the Year 2019." *Time*, December 11, 2019, 48–49, 50–67. Accessed February 25, 2020. https://time.com/
magazine/us/5748137/december-23rd-2019-vol-194-no-27-u-s/.

Fessler, Pam. "US Census Bureau Reports Poverty Rate Down, but Millions Still
Poor." NPR. September 10, 2019. Accessed February 14, 2020. https://www
.npr.org/2019/09/10/759512938/u-s-census-bureau-reports-poverty-rate-down
-but-millions-still-poor.

Flaxman, Seth, Sharad Goel, and Justin M. Rao. "Filter Bubbles, Echo Chambers,
and Online News Consumption." In "Party Polarization." Special issue. *Public
Opinion Quarterly, 80*, no. S1 (2016): 298–320.

Florentine, Sharon. "Everything You Need to Know about Generation Z." CIO.
June 20, 2018. Accessed June 19, 2019. https://www.cio.com/article/3282415/
everything-you-need-to-know-about-generation-z.html.

Fourtané, Susan. "Generation Alpha: The Children of the Millennial." Interesting
Engineering. December 18, 2018. Accessed May 1, 2020. https://interesting
engineering.com/generation-alpha-the-children-of-the-millennial.

Freire, Paulo. *Pedagogy of the Oppressed*. 30th anniversary ed. Translated by Myra
Bergman Ramos. New York: Continuum, 2000.

Frey, William H. "The US Will Become 'Minority White' in 2045, Census Projects."
Brookings. September 10, 2018. https://www.brookings.edu/blog/the-avenue/
2018/03/14/the-us-will-become-minority-white-in-2045-census-projects/.

Gallup. "'Pro-Choice' or 'Pro-Life,' 2018–2019 Demographic Tables." Gallup. Accessed February 18, 2020. https://news.gallup.com/poll/244709/pro-choice-pro
-life-2018-demographic-tables.aspx.

Gardner Institute. Accessed February 11, 2020. https://www.jngi.org/.

Geanous, Jacob. "Children Stage Mass-Walkout after Teachers Were Forced to Quit
for Being Gay." *Metro*, February 19, 2020. Accessed February 25, 2020. https://
metro.co.uk/2020/02/19/students-walk-class-catholic-school-forced-gay-teachers
-quit-12269247/.

Gerdes, Lindsey. *The Best Places to Launch a Career: Top Employers for Interns and
New College Grads*. New York: McGraw-Hill, 2008.

Giancola, Frank. "The Generation Gap: More Myth than Reality." *Human Resource Planning* 29, no. 4 (2006): 32.

Gilligan, Carol. *In a Different Voice: Psychological Theory and Women's Development*. 1982. Reprint, Cambridge, MA: Harvard University Press, 2016.

Gilsdorf, Ethan. "What Makes Superheroes So Super?" WBUR. March 25, 2016. https://www.wbur.org/artery/2016/03/25/what-makes-superheroes-so-super.

Goleman, Daniel. "What Makes a Leader?" In *HBR's 10 Must Reads on Emotional Intelligence*, 1–21. Boston: Harvard Business Review Press, 2015.

Goleman, Daniel, and Richard E. Boyatzis. "Emotional Intelligence Has 12 Elements. Which Do You Need to Work On?" *Harvard Business Review*, February 6, 2017. bit.ly/HRBEmotionalIntelligence.

Goodreads. "Popular Western Canon Books." Accessed October 29, 2020. https://www.goodreads.com/shelf/show/western-canon.

Gordinier, Jeff. *X Saves the World: How Generation X Got the Shaft but Can Still Keep Everything from Sucking*. New York: Viking, 2008.

Gray, John. *Men Are from Mars, Women Are from Venus: The Classic Guide to Understanding the Opposite Sex*. 1992. Reprint, New York: HarperCollins, 2012.

Green, Brent. *Marketing to Leading-Edge Baby Boomers*. Lincoln, NE: Writers Advantage, 2003.

Grynbaum, Michael M., and Tiffany Hsu. "Major Networks Cut Away from Trump's Baseless Fraud Claims." *New York Times*, November 5, 2020. Accessed November 6, 2020. https://www.nytimes.com/2020/11/05/business/media/ trump-tv.html.

Gutierrez, Jon, Luke Y. Thompson, and Andy Hughes. "The 6 Worst Jobs Wonder Woman Ever Had." Topless Robot. September 4, 2015. https://www.toplessrobot.com/2011/03/the_6_worst_jobs_wonder_woman_ever_had.php.

Hardy, Benjamin P. "The Most Potent Gen-Z Entrepreneurial Panel Assembled." Inc.com. August 25, 2018. Accessed January 21, 2020. https://www.inc.com/ benjamin-p-hardy/the-most-potent-gen-z-entrepreneurial-panel-assembled.html.

Hartzog-Mislock, Deenie, and Seeta Kanhai. "Meet 6 Gen Z Activists That Are Setting an Extraordinary Example." Refinery29. April 1, 2019. Accessed February 3, 2020. https://www.refinery29.com/en-us/gen-z-female-entrepreneurs.

Henson, Mary F. *Trends in the Income of Families and Persons in the United States 1947–1964*. Washington, DC: US Department of Commerce, Bureau of the Census, 1967.

Hess, Abigail. "Tuition at Public Colleges Has Increased in All 50 States over the Past 10 Years—Here's How Your State Compares." CNBC. October 24, 2019. Accessed February 14, 2020. https://www.cnbc.com/2019/10/24/college-costs -have-increased-in-all-50-states-over-the-past-10-years.html.

Hirsch, E. D., Jr. *Cultural Literacy: What Every American Needs to Know.* New York: Houghton-Mifflin, 1987.

Hirsh, Sophie. "13-Year-Old Vegan Climate Activist Genesis Butler Is on a Mission to Make the World a Kinder Place." GreenMatters. Accessed November 5, 2020, https://www.greenmatters.com/p/genesis-butler-vegan-climate-activist.

History. "Rosie the Riveter." Accessed August 31, 2014. http://www.history.com/topics/world-war-ii/rosie-the-riveter.

History.com Editors. "*Brown v. Board of Education.*" History. Updated February 21, 2020. Accessed February 21, 2020. https://www.history.com/topics/black-history/brown-v-board-of-education-of-topeka.

———. "Civil Rights Movement Timeline." History. Updated January 16, 2020. Accessed February 12, 2020. https://www.history.com/topics/civil-rights-movement/civil-rights-movement-timeline.

Holt, Brianna. "Gen-Zers on Tinder Want Someone to March With, Not Just Match With." Quartz. December 17, 2019. Accessed February 3, 2020. https://qz.com/1769311/gen-z-is-putting-social-justice-issues-on-tinder-profiles/.

Howe, Neil. "Don't Worry, America: Millennials Still Want to Marry." *Forbes*, March 25, 2014. Accessed September 29, 2014. https://www.forbes.com/sites/realspin/2014/03/25/dont-worry-america-millennials-still-want-to-marry/?sh=3802fd614035.

Howe, Neil, and William Strauss. *Millennials Rising: The Next Great Generation.* New York: Vintage Books, 2000.

Hulbert, Ann. "Look Who's Parenting." *New York Times*, July 4, 2004. http://www.nytimes.com/2004/07/04/magazine/04WWLN.html.

Jacobson, Beah, and Natalia Tramontana. "Seven Young Leaders Making Black History Today." America's Promise Alliance. February 8, 2018. Accessed February 14, 2020. https://www.americaspromise.org/news/seven-young-leaders-making-black-history-today.

Jennings, Jazz. "When I First Knew I Was Transgender." *Time*, May 31, 2016. Accessed February 14, 2020. https://time.com/4350574/jazz-jennings-transgender/.

Judd, Donald. "'I Want to Be Brave Like You': 9-Year-Old Asks Pete Buttigieg to Help Him Tell the World He's Gay." CNN. February 23, 2020. Accessed February 25, 2020. https://www.cnn.com/2020/02/23/politics/pete-buttigieg-denver-rally-moment/index.html.

Kabat-Zinn, Jon. "Guided Mindfulness Meditation Practices with Jon Kabat-Zinn." Mindfulnesscds.com. Accessed November 1, 2020. https://www.mindfulnesscds.com/.

Kahoot. "What Is Kahoot!?" Accessed February 6, 2020. https://kahoot.com/what-is-kahoot/.

Kantrowitz, Alan. "Twitter Will Allow Employees to Work at Home Forever." Buzzfeed. May 12, 2020. https://www.buzzfeednews.com/article/alexkantrowitz/twitter-will-allow-employees-to-work-at-home-forever.

Katz, Andrew. "Unrest in Virginia." *Time.* Accessed February 11, 2020. https://time.com/charlottesville-white-nationalist-rally-clashes/.

Kessler, Glenn, Salvador Rizzo, and Meg Kelly. "President Trump Made 16,241 False or Misleading Claims in His First Three Years." *Washington Post*, January 22, 2020. https://www.washingtonpost.com/politics/2020/01/20/president-trump-made-16241-false-or-misleading-claims-his-first-three-years/.

Khan Academy. "Second-Wave Feminism." Accessed February 12, 2020. https://www.khanacademy.org/humanities/us-history/postwarera/1960s-america/a/second-wave-feminism.

Khomami, Nadia. "#MeToo: How a Hashtag Became a Rallying Cry against Sexual Harassment." *Guardian*, October 20, 2017. Accessed February 25, 2020. https://www.theguardian.com/world/2017/oct/20/women-worldwide-use-hashtag-metoo-against-sexual-harassment.

Kingston, Anne. "Get Ready for Generation Z." *Maclean's*, July 21, 2014, 42–45. https://www.macleans.ca/society/life/get-ready-for-generation-z/.

Kupperschmidt, Betty R. 2000. "Multigeneration Employees: Strategies for Effective Management." *Health Care Manager* 19, no. 1 (2000): 65–76. Accessed April 10, 2020. https://europepmc.org/article/med/11183655. DOI: 10.1097/00126450-200019010-00011.

Lange, Julian E., Abdul Ali, Candida G. Brush, Andrew C. Corbett, Donna J. Kelley, Phillip H. Kim, and Mahdi Majbouri. *2017 United States Report: Global Entrepreneurship Monitor: National Entrepreneurial Assessment for the United States of America.* Babson Park, MA: Babson College, 2018. Accessed January 21, 2020. https://www.babson.edu/media/babson/site-assets/content-assets/academics/centers-and-institutes/the-arthur-m-blank-center-for-entrepreneurship/global-research/GEM_USA_2017.pdf.

Lashbrooke, Barnaby. "Want More from Generation Z? Mentor, Don't Manage Them." *Forbes*, June 24, 2019. https://www.forbes.com/sites/barnabylashbrooke/2019/06/21/want-more-from-generation-z-mentor-dont-manage-them/#52f6ae505530.

Leane, Rob. "8 Superhero Games in Development or Rumored." Den of Geek. January 10, 2020. Accessed February 19, 2020. https://www.denofgeek.com/us/games/278501/upcoming-superhero-games.

Lee, Andrew M. I. "No Child Left Behind (NCLB): What You Need to Know." Understood. Accessed February 10, 2020. https://www.understood.org/en/school

-learning/your-childs-rights/basics-about-childs-rights/no-child-left-behind-nclb
-what-you-need-to-know.

Lee, Lauren. "California Teen Donates More than 150 Coronavirus Sanitation Kits to the Homeless. Now She Wants Your Help to Distribute More." CNN. March 19, 2020. https://www.cnn.com/2020/03/19/us/teen-donates-sanitization-kits-to -homeless-iyw-trnd/index.html.

Levy, Alison Rose. "The Deepwater Horizon Oil Spill Was a Cover-Up, Not a Cleanup." TruthDig. February 17, 2020. Accessed February 18, 2020. https:// www.truthdig.com/articles/the-deepwater-horizon-oil-spill-was-a-cover-up-not-a -cleanup/.

Lewis, Jerry M., and Thomas R. Hensley. "The May 4 Shootings at Kent State University: The Search for Historical Accuracy." Kent State University. Accessed February 10, 2020. https://www.kent.edu/may-4-historical-accuracy.

Linder, Douglas O. "*State v. John Scopes* ('The Monkey Trial')." July 10, 2000. Accessed August 31, 2014. http://law2.umkc.edu/faculty/projects/ftrials/scopes/ evolut.htm.

Lindsell-Roberts, Sheryl. "Bridging the Multigenerational Divide." In *New Rules for Today's Workplace*. Boston: Houghton Mifflin Harcourt, 2011.

Lukacs, John. *A Short History of the Twentieth Century*. Cambridge, MA: Belknap Press, 2013.

Lukianoff, Greg, and Jonathan Haidt. *The Coddling of the American Mind: How Good Intentions and Bad Ideas Are Setting Up a Generation for Failure*. New York: Penguin Press, 2018.

Luttrell, Regina. "Social Networking Sites in the Public Relations Classroom: A Mixed Methods Analysis of Undergraduate Learning Outcomes Using Word-Press, Facebook, and Twitter." PhD diss. California Institute of Integral Studies, 2012.

Luttrell, Regina, and Natalia Flores. "Why Diversity and Inclusion Warrant PR's Rapt Attention." *PR Daily*, October 3, 2019. https://www.prdaily.com/why -diversity-and-inclusion-warrant-prs-rapt-attention/.

Luttrell, Regina, and Karen McGrath. *The Millennial Mindset: Unraveling Fact from Fiction*. Lanham, MD: Rowman & Littlefield, 2015.

Lynch, Matthew. "7 Examples of Project-Based Learning Activities." Tech Advocate. October 19, 2017. Accessed February 26, 2020. https://www.thetech edvocate.org/7-examples-project-based-learning-activities/.

Maayan. "Queeng Playing Cards." Indiegogo. Accessed January 28, 2020. https:// www.indiegogo.com/projects/queeng-playing-cards#/.

Manoff, Jill. "5 Gen-Z Influencers You Need to Know." Digiday. June 6, 2019. Accessed February 6, 2020. https://digiday.com/marketing/5-gen-z-influencers-know/.

Marzullo, Dan. "How to Motivate Generation Z at Work." Workest. October 15, 2019. Accessed March 23, 2020. https://www.zenefits.com/workest/how-to -motivate-generation-z-at-work/.

Mastin, Luke. "Introduction." Basics of Philosophy. Accessed January 16, 2020. https://www.philosophybasics.com/branch_ethics.html.

McCrindle. "Gen Z and Gen Alpha Infographic Update." February 15, 2020. https://mccrindle.com.au/insights/blogarchive/gen-z-and-gen-alpha-infographic -update/.

McMilan, Graeme. "S.H.I.E.L.D. 101: Everything You Need to Know About Marvel's Spy Agency." Wired, September 24, 2013. Accessed February 19, 2020. https://www.wired.com/2013/09/s-h-i-e-l-d-101-faq/.

McPherson, Jim. "Media History Timeline." 2002. Accessed September 1, 2014. http://www.webpages.uidaho.edu/jamm445hart/timeline.htm.

Meyer, David S. "One Year after the Parkland Shooting, Is the #NeverAgain Movement on Track to Succeed?" Washington Post, February 14, 2019. Accessed January 18, 2020. http://thewashingtonpost.com/news/monkey-cage/wp/ 2019/02/14/one-year-after-the-parkland-shooting-is-the-neveragain-movement -on-track-to-succeed/.

MilkFoundation.org. Accessed September 1, 2014. http://milkfoundation.org/.

Mindful. Accessed November 1, 2020. https://www.mindful.org/.

MindTools. "Emotional Intelligence in Leadership: Learning How to Be More Aware." Accessed February 24, 2020. https://www.mindtools.com/pages/article/ newLDR_45.htm.

MirandaRights.org. "Miranda Rights." Accessed September 1, 2014. http://www .mirandarights.org/.

National Archives and Records Administration. "19th Amendment to the U.S. Constitution: Women's Right to Vote." Accessed August 31, 2014. https://www .archives.gov/historical-docs/19th-amendment.

National Education Association. "Code of Ethics." September 14, 2020. https:// www.nea.org/resource-library/code-ethics.

National Oceanic and Atmospheric Administration. "2019 Was 2nd Hottest Year on Record for Earth Say NOAA, NASA." January 15, 2020. Accessed February 21, 2020. https://www.noaa.gov/news/2019-was-2nd-hottest-year-on-record-for -earth-say-noaa-nasa.

Natural Resources Defense Council. "The Silent Spring." Accessed August 28, 2014. http://www.nrdc.org/health/pesticides/hcarson.asp.

Newman, Kira M. "Free Mindfulness Apps Worthy of Your Attention." Mindful. November 18, 2019. Accessed February 5, 2020. https://www.mindful.org/free -mindfulness-apps-worthy-of-your-attention/.

Ng, Eddy S. W., Linda Schweitzer, and Sean T. Lyons. "New Generation, Great Expectations: A Field Study of the Millennial Generation." *Journal of Business and Psychology* 25, no. 2 (2010): 281–92. https://doi.org/10.1007/s10869-010 -9159-4.

Ninjago Wiki. "Digiverse." Accessed January 29, 2020. https://ninjago.fandom .com/wiki/Digiverse.

The Nobel Prize. "Malala Yousafzai: Facts." Accessed February14, 2020. https:// www.nobelprize.org/prizes/peace/2014/yousafzai/facts/.

Northouse, Peter G. *Leadership: Theory and Practice.* 6th ed. Thousand Oaks, CA: Sage, 2013.

Ohlheiser, Abby. "The Woman behind 'Me Too' Knew the Power of the Phrase When She Created It—10 Years Ago." *Washington Post*, October 19, 2017. Accessed February 25, 2020. https://www.washingtonpost.com/news/the-intersect/ wp/2017/10/19/the-woman-behind-me-too-knew-the-power-of-the-phrase-when -she-created-it-10-years-ago/.

O'Neal, Kennedy. "Super Kennedy—Piggybank (Official Music Video)." Video, 2:01. January 1, 2020. Accessed February 24, 2020.https://www.youtube.com/ watch?v=-gO_spXX-Q.

Ortiz-Ospina, Esteban, and Diana Beltekian. "Why Do Women Live Longer than Men?" Our World in Data. August 14, 2018. Accessed February 20, 2020. https://ourworldindata.org/why-do-women-live-longer-than-men.

Oxford Learner's Dictionaries. "Persona." Accessed March 9, 2020. https://www .oxfordlearnersdictionaries.com/us/definition/english/persona?q=persona.

Pandit, Vivek. *We Are Generation Z: How Identity, Attitudes, and Perspectives Are Shaping Our Future.* Dallas: Brown Books, 2015.

Pasquarelli, Adrienne, and E. J. Schultz. "Move Over Gen Z, Generation Alpha Is the One to Watch." *Ad Age*, January 22, 2019. Accessed April 30, 2020. https:// adage.com/article/cmo-strategy/move-gen-z-generation-alpha-watch/316314.

Patel, Deep. "10 Gen Z Experts You Should Be Following." *Forbes*, July 6, 2017. Accessed January 21, 2020. https://www.forbes.com/sites/deeppatel/2017/07/06/10 -gen-z-experts-you-should-be-following/#404fa68e69cc.

Paterson, Jim. "Class of 2017: The Good, the Bad, and What's Next." *Journal of College Admission*, no. 234 (Winter 2017): 45–46. Accessed February 25, 2020. https://files.eric.ed.gov/fulltext/EJ1142215.pdf.

Perano, Ursula. "Meet Generation Alpha, the 9-Year-Olds Shaping Our Future." Axios. August 8, 2019. Accessed, May 1, 2020. https://www.axios.com/generation -alpha-millennial-children-63438b10-6817-483e-8472-38810df77880.html.

Pitofsky, Marina. "Child Pays Off Lunch Debt for Over 120 Classmates with Stand Selling Cider, Cocoa and Cookies." *Hill*, December 17, 2019. Accessed February

20, 2020. https://thehill.com/blogs/blog-briefing-room/news/474950-5-year-old
-pays-off-lunch-debt-for-over-120-classmates-with.

Politifact. Accessed November 1, 2020. https://www.politifact.com/.

Pruitt, Sarah. "What Happened at the Stonewall Riots? A Timeline of the 1969
Uprising." History. Updated June 28, 2019. Accessed February 12, 2020. https://
www.history.com/news/stonewall-riots-timeline.

Rainer, Thom S., and Jess W. Rainer. *The Millennials: Connecting to America's
Largest Generation*. Nashville: B&H, 2011.

Raymond, Nicholas. "Every Upcoming DC TV Show." Screen Rant. October 31,
2019. Accessed February 19, 2020. https://screenrant.com/dc-tv-shows-upcoming/.

Red Tail Squadron. "A Brief History of the Tuskegee Airmen." Accessed August
31, 2014. http://www.redtail.org/the-airmen-a-brief-history/.

Redden, Elizabeth. "Young Voters Preferred Biden—With 1 Exception." Inside Higher
Ed. Last modified November 5, 2020. Accessed November 6, 2020. https://inside
highered.com/news/2020/11/05/analysis-sheds-first-light-youth-voting-trends.

Satara, Alyssa. "In 2 Sentences Elon Musk Explains Why the Key to Success Is
Failure." Inc.com. April 30, 2018. Accessed February 6, 2020. https://www
.inc.com/alyssa-satara/in-2-sentences-elon-musk-explains-why-key-to-success-is
-failure.html.

Scagliotti, John, dir. *After Stonewall*. Narrated by Melissa Etheridge. New York:
First Run Features, 2005. DVD.

Schultz, Jeff. "How Much Data Is Created on the Internet Each Day?" *Micro Focus*
(blog). June 8, 2019. Accessed February 24, 2020. https://blog.microfocus.com/
how-much-data-is-created-on-the-internet-each-day/.

Seemiller, Corey, and Meghan Grace. *Generation Z: A Century in the Making*. New
York: Routledge, 2019.

———. *Generation Z Goes to College*. San Francisco: Jossey-Bass, 2016.

Segal, Jeanne, Melinda Smith, Lawrence Robinson, and Jennifer Shubin. "Improving
Emotional Intelligence (EQ)." HelpGuide. October 2019. bit.ly/HelpGuideEQ.

Shearer, Laura M. "Marvel and DC Superhero Movies since 2000." IMDb. Updated
September 26, 2012. Accessed February 19, 2020. https://www.imdb.com/list/
ls008923275/.

Steinmetz, Katy. "Move Over, Millennials: How Generation Z Is Disrupting Work as
We Know It." *Time*, December 15, 2017. https://time.com/5066641/generation
-z-disruption/.

Sterbenz, Christina. "Here's Who Comes after Generation Z—and They'll Be the
Most Transformative Age Group Ever." *Business Insider*, December 5, 2015.
Accessed April 28, 2020. http://www.buinessinsider.com/generation-alpha-2014
-7-2.

Stillman, David, and Jonah Stillman. *Gen Z @ Work: How the Next Generation Is Transforming the Workplace.* New York: HarperCollins, 2017.

StopBullying.gov. Accessed November 1, 2020. https://www.stopbullying.gov/.

Stout, Maureen. *The Feel-Good Curriculum: The Dumbing Down of America's Kids in the Name of Self-Esteem.* Boston: Da Capo Press, 2007.

Student Press Law Center. "College Press Freedom and Censorship." Accessed February 21, 2020. https://splc.org/college/.

Tapscott, Don. *Grown Up Digital: How the Net Generation Is Changing Your World.* New York: McGraw Hill, 2009.

Taylor, Paul, and George Gao. "Generation X: America's Neglected 'Middle Child.'" Pew Research Center. June 5, 2014. Accessed August 15, 2014. https://www.pewresearch.org/fact-tank/2014/06/05/generation-x-americas-neglected -middle-child/.

Taylor, Paul, and Scott Keeter, eds. *Millennials: Confident. Connected. Open to Change.* Washington, DC: Pew Research Center, February 2010. Accessed April 10, 2020. http://www.pewsocialtrends.org/files/2010/10/millennials-confident -connected-open-to-change.pdf.

Thomas, Susan Gregory. "A Teacher's Guide to Generation X Parents." *Edutopia,* January 19, 2010. Accessed August 15, 2014. https://www.edutopia.org/ generation-x-parents-relationships-guide.

Tobin, Thomas J., and Kirsten T. Behling. *Reach Everyone, Teach Everyone: Universal Design for Learning in Higher Education.* Morgantown: University of West Virginia Press, 2018.

Tracy, Mark. "In Haste to Confirm Kobe Bryant News, News Media Stumbles." *New York Times,* January 27, 2020. Accessed February 2, 2020. https://www .nytimes.com/2020/01/27/business/tmz-kobe.html.

Travel Technology and Solutions. "Who Is Generation Alpha and Are They Going to Change the Travel Industry?" May 10, 2019. Accessed April 28, 2020. http://www.tts.com/blog/who-is-generation-alpha-and-are-they-going-to-change -the-travel-industry/.

Troitino, Christina. "Why Taco Bell's Viral $100,000 Salary Test Isn't Ridiculous." *Forbes,* January 10, 2020. Accessed February 21, 2020. https://www.forbes.com/ sites/christinatroitino/2020/01/10/why-taco-bells-viral-100000-salary-test-isnt -ridiculous/#e626e7831f08.

Turk, Victoria. "Understanding Generation Alpha." *Wired,* October 17, 2017. Accessed April 28, 2020. https://www.wired.co.uk/article/understanding -generation-alpha.

Turner, Anthony. "Generation Z and Social Interest." *Journal of Individual Psychology,* 71, no. 2 (Summer 2015): 108. https://doi.org/10.1353/jip.2015.0021.

Twenge, Jean M. *Generation Me*. Rev. ed. New York: Apria Books, 2014.

———. *iGen: Why Today's Super-Connected Kids Are Growing Up Less Rebellious, More Tolerant, Less Happy—and Completely Unprepared for Adulthood: And What It Means for the Rest of Us*. New York: Atria Books, 2018.

Underwood, Chuck. *Generational Imperative: Understanding Generational Differences in the Workplace, Marketplace and Living Room*. Miamisburg, OH: Generational Imperative, 2007.

United Nations Joint Staff Pension Fund. "Traditionalists, Baby Boomers, Generation X, Generation Y (and Generation Z) Working Together." New York Secretariat Headquarters. Accessed April 10, 2020. http://aspringer.weebly.com/up loads/1/3/6/4/1364481/designing_recruitment_selection___talent_management _model_tailored_to_meet_unjspfs_business_development_nee.pdf.

United States Courts. "History—*Brown v. Board of Education*." Accessed August 31, 2014. http://www.uscourts.gov/educational-resources/get-involved/federal -court-activities/brown-board-education-re-enactment/history.aspx.

US Census Bureau. "USA QuickFacts." July 8, 2014. Accessed August 14, 2014. https://www.census.gov/quickfacts/fact/table/US/INC110218.

US Equal Employment Opportunity Commission. "The Law." Accessed September 1, 2014. http://www.eeoc.gov/eeoc/history/35th/thelaw/.

US History. "*Roe v. Wade* and Its Impact." Accessed September 1, 2014. http:// www.ushistory.org/us/57d.asp.

US NRC. "Backgrounder on the Three Mile Island Accident." Accessed September 1, 2014. http://www.nrc.gov/reading-rm/doc-collections/fact-sheets/3mile-isle .html.

Vox. "Sexual Harassment and Assault Allegations List." Updated January 9, 2019. Accessed January 28, 2020. https://www.vox.com/a/sexual-harassment-assault -allegations-list.

Villa, Denise, Jason Dorsey, and Elli Denison. *The State of Gen Z 2018*. Austin, TX: Center for Generational Kinetics, Fall 2018. Accessed June 19, 2019. https://genhq .com/wp-content/uploads/2018/10/State-of-Gen-Z-2018.pdf?inf_contact_key=b4 b0f67ed8ed53ee3bb1e8019e212ecd447d8eaa43673fdaa114662fd31ef250.

Walsh, James D. "The Coming Disruption: Scott Galloway Predicts a Handful of Elite Cyborg Universities Will Soon Monopolize Higher Education." Intelligencer. May 11, 2020. https://nymag.com/intelligencer/2020/05/scott-galloway -future-of-college.html.

Watson, Heather. "How Obsessed Is Gen Z with Mobile Technology?" Center for Generational Kinetics. Accessed February 13, 2020. https://genhq.com/how -obsessed-is-gen-z-with-mobile-technology/.

Wattenberg, Ben. "Stock Market Crash." PBS: The First Measured Century. Accessed August 31, 2014. https://www.pbs.org/fmc/timeline/estockmktcrash.htm.

Watts, Jonathan. "Antarctic Temperature Rises above 20C for First Time on Record." *Guardian*, February 13, 2020. Accessed February 20, 2020. https://www.theguardian.com/world/2020/feb/13/antarctic-temperature-rises-above-20c-first-time-record.

Weaver, Hilary. "Here Is Every Superhero Movie Coming Out for the Foreseeable Future." *Esquire*, October 23, 2019. Accessed February 19, 2020. https://www.esquire.com/entertainment/movies/a29551205/upcoming-new-superhero-movies/.

Weisman, Aly. "Here's How TMZ Got the Name TMZ." *Business Insider*, July 31, 2014. Accessed February 2, 2020. https://www.businessinsider.com/what-does-tmz-stand-for-2014-7.

Weltzien, Friedrich. "Masque-ulinities: Changing Dress as a Display of Masculinity in the Superhero Genre." *Fashion Theory* 9, no. 2 (2005): 229–50. https://doi.org/10.2752/136270405778051374.

Western, Dan. "The Top 22 Motivational Superhero Quotes." WealthyGorilla. Accessed February 26, 2020. https://wealthygorilla.com/top-22-motivational-superhero-quotes/.

Whistle, Wesley. "A Look at Millennial Student Debt." *Forbes*, October 3, 2019. Accessed October 4, 2019. https://www.forbes.com/sites/wesleywhistle/2019/10/03/a-look-at-millennial-student-debt/#67a212a2437e.

White, Abbey. "Fans Praise Jennifer Lopez for Puerto Rican Pride, Pro-Immigration Statement during Super Bowl Halftime." *Hollywood Reporter*, February 2, 2020. Accessed February 3, 2020. https://www.hollywoodreporter.com/news/super-bowl-halftime-jennifer-lopez-praised-subtle-immigration-statements-1275653.

Wikipedia. "Trolley Problem." Accessed March 29, 2020. https://en.wikipedia.org/wiki/Trolley_problem.

Williams, Alex. "Meet Alpha: The Next 'Next' Generation." *New York Times*, September 19, 2015. https://www.nytimes.com/2015/09/19/fashion/meet-alpha-the-next-next-generation.html.

Wines, Michael. "What Is Gerrymandering? And Why Did the Supreme Court Rule on It?" *New York Times*, June 27, 2019. Accessed February 21, 2020. https://www.nytimes.com/2019/06/27/us/what-is-gerrymandering.html.

Winograd, Michael. "It's Official: Millennials Realigned American Politics in 2008." Huffington Post. November 17, 2008. Accessed September 5, 2014. https://www.huffpost.com/entry/its-official-millennials_b_144357?guccounter=1&guce_referrer=aHR0cHM6Ly93d3cuZ29vZ2xlLmNvbS88&guce_referrer_sig=AQAAADnGxfTSVlZJhWiJm2I5jBpHkDCdrMlxJZt-Gk7uOm0HspM

6apiPPtLyR-THFkE2II8Xpz8xHlyQ98S98Ku1hrAQ0Rkr9IWPIei2BIBAcIa
EvSt5PqGHM7B-EhS5JLKohvjgs2ldAOp2Q7_Z4TXGNGUmcsF0cnEcu
0LP0VHi5wHf.

Workplace Bullying Institute. Accessed November 1, 2020. https://www.workplace
bullying.org.

World Economic Forum. Annual meeting, Davos-Klosters, Switzerland, January
20–23, 2016. Accessed October 27, 2020. https://newclimateeconomy.net/
content/world-economic-forum-annual-meeting-2016.

Zapata, Kimberly. "Meet Generation Alpha. Here's How Their Lives Will Be Different than Previous Generations." BestLife. August 13, 2019. Accessed April 28,
2020. http://bestlifeonline.com/generation-alpha-facts/.

Zarra, Ernest J. *Helping Parents Understand the Minds and Hearts of Generation Z.*
Lanham, MD: Rowman & Littlefield, 2017.

Zemke, Ron, Claire Raines, and Bob Filipczak. *Generations at Work: Managing the
Clash of Boomers, Gen Xers, and Gen Yers in the Workplace.* 2nd ed. New York:
AMACOM/American Management Association, 2013.

Zraick, Karen. "22 States Considered Eliminating the 'Tampon Tax' This Year.
Here's What Happened." *New York Times,* July 12, 2019. Accessed February 3,
2020. https://www.nytimes.com/2019/07/12/us/tampon-tax.html.

INDEX

ABOUT THE
AUTHORS

Regina Luttrell, PhD, is the associate dean for research and creativity activity, the director of the W20 Emerging Insights Lab, and an assistant professor of public relations and social media at the S. I. Newhouse School of Public Communications at Syracuse University, where she researches, publishes, and discusses public relations, social media for strategic communication, Gen-Alpha, Gen-Z, and the millennial generation, as well as the intersection of social media within society. Luttrell's research has been published in academic journals and books. She is the author or coauthor of *Social Media: How to Engage, Share, and Connect*; *The Millennial Mindset: Unraveling Fact from Fiction*; *Brew Your Business: The Ultimate Craft Beer Playbook*; *Public Relations Campaigns: An Integrated Approach*; *The PR Agency Handbook*; and *A Practical Guide to Ethics in Public Relations*. Most recently, she edited and contributed to *Trump Tweets: The World Reacts; Understanding What Is Relevant and Why?* and *American Democracy: Influence, Activism, and Misinformation in the Social Era*. Superpower: As a fierce and proud feminist, she advocates for the equality and rights of all women.

Karen McGrath, PhD, is a professor, author, scholar, and superhero wannabe who pursues tasks with verve, "pows," and "bams" without a cape. She coauthored *The Millennial Mindset: Unraveling Fact from Fiction* (2015) and *Brew Your Business: The Ultimate Craft Beer Playbook* (2017). She has also published analyses of marginalized groups in pop culture, including Archie Comics, Marvel Comics, and *The Big Bang Theory*. Her latest publication, "Leveraging Esports in Higher Education," in Ryan Rogers's *Understanding Esports: An Introduction to the Global Phenomenon* (2019), demonstrates her interest in keeping up with higher education and generational trends.

CPSIA information can be obtained
at www.ICGtesting.com
Printed in the USA
LVHW111800160421
684726LV00001B/39